IMMEDIATE EXPERIENTIAL COGNITION

By Julian Hamer

Dedicated to my beautiful wife Ellen

IMMEDIATE EXPERIENTIAL COGNITION
The Inherent, Human Capacity of Immediate Engagement

by Julian Hamer

Contents

1. The Qualitative Maturation of the Soul

If a worthwhile objective is clearly defined and the effective means of its ultimate attainment is reasonable, the practical application of human resolve confidently ensures success. Based on these considerations, when the selected intention is peace of mind whereby the human moribund mentality is superseded by a successive ethos, already our purpose is specific, and it only remains to continue earnestly in the most expedient manner towards certain accomplishment.

Human evolution concerns the substantive development of the soul towards an upright and reputable autonomy inspirited through the ethos of integrity and goodwill. Consequently, when the human soul discovers that it is able to qualitatively advance, it must do so because regression is not a viable option in terms of essential progress. Indeed, any meaningful maturation that has been hitherto accomplished is subsequently renounced upon the indulgence of an ethical reversal. Similarly, developmental inertia implies that we continue to reiterate established dispositional patterns even though they may work against an imperative transformative impetus. Accordingly, in the same manner that it is for a developing child, the only realistic option is to persevere.

Upon the increasingly significant occurrence of individual awakening towards respective independence, a

1

commensurate mandatory responsibility towards the ethical enhancement of the human constitution has become imperative. For example, if we consider the lamentable circumstances of human affairs upon the increase of privilege but without established responsibility, clearly the prospects of the equitable resolution of human challenges remain remote. That is to say, without an established ethos of integrity and goodwill, prosperity and amenity of themselves are meaningless.

Ultimately, there is neither a realistic alternative nor practical escape from the necessity of the crucial evolutionary establishment of a successive, human frame of mind. There is only procrastination against inevitable soul-maturation. Providentially, qualitative progress pertains to the accommodation of an already extant, progressive ethos and not to the development of a humanly constituted morality. Indeed, the effective transformation of the psyche is not accomplished upon the strength of existing mortal resources because the indispensable, advanced disposition does not originate within the present human constitution. Consequently, the mind must become reconstituted upon a hitherto unfamiliar foundation through the agency of an external, exemplary mandate.

That is to say, if the objective is clear and the means whereby it is accomplished is understood, peace of mind is attainable through the action of openhearted sincerity and receptivity towards the immanent principle of the human successive nature that resides contiguously to the human soul. Nevertheless, when we are uncertain of an objective, the search for the practical means towards betterment remains a moot consideration. Consequently, if humanity fails to discover the supernal exemplar through openhearted sincerity because we are unaware of the imperative task before us, we witness the distressing implications of ignorance at every turn in the form of cultural decline and creative stagnation. Notwithstanding that everything necessary is already prepared towards qualitative human improvement, nevertheless, we remain within a state of evolutionary inertia until we wholeheartedly participate in the inauguration of a successive dispositional ethos.

If the priority of the qualitative betterment of the soul is misunderstood and regarded with little relevance, and overlooked as the primary objective of human evolution, all other devotional measures and practices are reduced to insignificance. Nevertheless, we may not realize that through determined endeavor, inadvertently the ethical standard of an individual is improved even upon as little as the heartfelt expression of goodwill.

For example, when a person wholeheartedly desires to release another from bitter resentment and animosity, by the motion of forgiveness the heart inevitably opens to the immanent supernal whereby the charitable soul spontaneously renders itself susceptible to

3

the ingress of the corrective influence of the exemplary nature. Thereby, through the sincere expression of inspired magnanimity within the heart, the soul of the well-wisher is itself qualitatively improved.

In view of the above example, we recognize that all significant, dispositional improvement commences within the heart. Needless to say, it is also from the endorsement and cultivation of acrimony that a dysfunctional mentality became established in the first place. Accordingly, both contrition and forgiveness are successive approaches towards dispositional amelioration, but clemency towards others is of itself a meaningful expression of character, with a reciprocal cleansing effect upon both the sponsor and the recipient. Indeed, the transaction of forgiveness benefits both sides because thereby, in a sense, the bestower serves as a fortuitous agency of the supernal will upon the collective, human psyche.

Thus, the desire to overcome an unworkable psychology and the aspiration towards a wholesome disposition, is indicative of progress in terms of the qualitative development of the soul. However, these things are of no avail unless they are completed through the communion of openhearted sincerity towards the immanent, supernal nature. In other words, the amelioration of the human soul is not accomplished by dilettante affirmation but through the vastly more profound medium of wholehearted vulnerability towards the immanent presence. Thereby, that which is beyond the extent of human will to achieve, may be unequivocally concluded by the influence of consummate wisdom and goodwill upon the respective heart.

Hence, clearly apparent is the necessity of the relinquishment of human control towards the accomplishment of a dispositional transformation because a dysfunctional mentality cannot self-ameliorate. In other words, the psyche cannot reconstruct according to unknown standards but must favorably prepare itself in order that the transformation of the mind by holy intervention may take place.

Therefore, through openhearted sincerity and the yielding of control, we allow whatever measures supernal wisdom deems appropriate to impress and supersede the extant, self-circumscribed mentality. Upon this understanding, we recognize that we are dealing with the entrenched psychology of the human subconscious mind and not merely behavioralism. Consequently, it is through deepest sincerity of heart that the remediation of the soul is inaugurated, but it is through supernal agency that the actual transformation of the moribund disposition is accomplished.

2. Straightforward Cognition

In order that the substance of the previous chapter may be empirically verified and the significance of individual, dispositional improvement be properly understood, we do not have to rely on either faith or divine revelation. That is, essential things can be directly experienced and tried individually for their authenticity. Indeed, every human being innately possesses the capacity to engage circumstances originally, and through the temporary restraint of conventional reasoning we thereby discover the intrinsic significance of things through straightforward cognition.

On the surface, it may seem that the distinction between an experientially verified condition, and the hypothetical or imaginary construct, is self-evident and readily determinable. However, in practice, thinking is as inconsistent as the extent of human consciousness at a particular moment. Consequently, at intervals, a person may be either objectively or speculatively preoccupied, and remain unconscious of the disparity.

Thus, in terms of real and unreal, while the difference appears conceptually obvious, nevertheless, experientially, real is a condition of authenticity and anything less than real does not actually exist. In point of fact, there remains only the real or nothing. In other words, knowledge discovered through direct cognition potentially exceeds in significance the hypothetical construct through the instantaneity of the approach. That is to say, immediate cognition, depending on the integrity of the practice, exceeds conceptual thinking through the direct experience of circumstances.

Furthermore, if, for a moment, we consider ordinary consciousness, we know from personal experience that most human thinking is subliminal and nearly all discourse is tainted by a subconscious agenda. It is true that the intellect may follow a reasonable, logical progression depending on the discipline and capability of the thinker, but through partiality and mental abstraction from the actual event, the possibility of dispassionate reflection remains remote. Consequently, even the most calculated and studied approach towards the intellectual acquisition of existential knowledge is insufficient in terms of definitive understanding because it necessarily occurs indirectly from the incident.

The reason for this difficulty is that the intellect serves as an obliquely operating faculty without the possibility of straightforward engagement. Conversely, direct cognition is the prerogative of an entity, while rationale is a mental aptitude without intrinsic distinction. Consequently, it follows that to the degree that the usual indirect approaches are restrained, the human being assumes untrammeled cognitive access.

By means of the practice of immediate cognition described above, the researcher promptly recognizes the immanent existence of a physically imperceptible magnitude that modifies an otherwise bland physicality with meaning. However, through a long-established conviction of the exclusive significance of the material portion of things, skepticism concerning the existence of an immanent, substantive volume is predictable, and the discerning reader is not easily persuaded otherwise by mere rhetoric. Nevertheless, the alternative narrow view of exclusive physicalism that offers only a shallow perspective towards life might at least serve as a stimulus towards further openminded research.

Nevertheless, the essential significance of things is meaningful while the transient remains the more superficial, subordinate countenance. Unfortunately, we become preoccupied with dependent, subsequent circumstances at the expense of the original principle through a failure of perspective. Consequently, the inconsequential and least profound presentation occupies our attention notwithstanding that it remains essentially shallow and transient. Nevertheless, if we wish to discover the considerable proportion of things, we can do so through an adjustment of perspective away from the superficial, cursory view towards the essential vantage of immediacy.

However, an abstract, philosophical standpoint is qualitatively incommensurate with the condition of directly ascertained existence because the former is always speculative. That is to say, conceptions and suppositions only exist potentially as possible explanations while immanently extant situations occur emphatically and definitively. Accordingly, the immediate experience of a phenomenon is wholly distinct from a merely conceptual position concerning it. This means that the direct approach will necessarily recognize a thing in the condition in which it actually exists.

Invariably the intellect operates indirectly and remotely from an original situation, and, as a function, it is unable to experience because it does not possess the existential quiddity of the human entity. Consequently, an obliquely conceived philosophy or doctrine explaining life cannot justifiably take precedence over directly ascertained knowledge. That is to say, only the intrinsic identity of a person is capable of direct, cognitive contact, whereas an organic faculty or a biological instrument serves as an intermediary, interpretive component that cannot otherwise directly engage a phenomenon.

The intellect, as an organic function, necessarily evaluates information indirectly because it is without personal distinction. However, the essential identity of the human being, as a uniquely integral entity, is able to engage something immediately and experientially. That is, while the indirect operation of the intellect must inevitably, obliquely evaluate the particulars of phenomena, the intrinsic, human distinction is capable of straightforward cognition.

Consequently, reason and imagination work closely in order to advance our understanding, and postulate and explore hypothetical possibilities endeavoring to resolve a question through rationale.

Nonetheless, an abstract hypothesis remains fallible regardless even of common consensus unless it is demonstrated to be authentic in practice. In other words, the proof of a position through rationale is insufficient qualification of the authenticity of something because proof befitting mathematical demonstration, remains inconclusive when applied to reason. That is, reason is mathematically imprecise, and the logical deduction of information and the application of the imagination towards the possibility of greater understanding is inevitably an inexact approach. Indeed, compared with knowledge derived through immediate engagement, abstract assessment is only a remote semblance.

Put another way, even though argument simulates mathematical procedure, it cannot arrive at a definitive resolution because it deals with ideas and not calculable quantities. Consequently, the researcher endeavors to quantify phenomena in order that, through transcription, physical properties may be reduced to a mathematical equivalence and be rendered calculable, alike to an equation.

Unfortunately, when dealing with existential conditions, those properties that are readily quantified are necessarily tangible and, consequently, do not represent the entirety of diversely expressed phenomena. Overlooked is the intangible, qualitative significance of

11

things, inherent to every object and circumstance. Consequently, a purely material definition inevitably fails to correspond with real life as we experience it directly. Furthermore, if a philosophical projection is constructed and extended solely upon the quantifiable factors of existence, the resulting representation will defy commonsense through an insufficiency of profundity and inadequacy in terms of perspective.

For example, the essential existence of a phenomenon as a continuum is insufficiently portrayed merely by the obviously transient, physical appearance. But a quietly restrained, objective mind discerns the intrinsic connotation of things. Therefore, when, through a philosophical slight-of-hand, the limited capability of the intellect is extended to supersede experientially derived knowledge as the sole arbiter of authenticity, it must, inevitably, dispense with the intangible qualitative proportion. But without qualities, values and intrinsic identities the submitted representation fails to resemble reality as we know it from our own experience.

That is to say, the exclusive, quantifiable properties of phenomena are invariably material because if something possesses a more profound significance than the obvious, it cannot be physically justified and proven. Furthermore, if, subsequently, the physical appearances of phenomena are imagined to comprise the full extent of existence, then the resultant philosophical construct is bound to conflict with the findings of the direct

12

encounter. Consequently, in terms of establishing a sound relationship towards existence, it is important that we heed the discrepancy because therein lies the deceit of materialistic Western philosophy.

Intangible qualities, values and intrinsic significances comprise the qualitative dimension of existence. But they can only be recognized experientially. Usually, they are evaluated through the human feeling nature, which is inevitably and of necessity, subjective.

Therefore, it is scarcely remarkable that the materialist turns a dismissive blind-eye to the significance of the qualitative dimension of existence because otherwise the established physically exclusive explanation of existence would be found seriously insufficient.

Predictably, subjectively derived information is incommensurate with methodically reasoned data founded upon physical properties. But if something cannot be precisely evaluated in physical terms, it does not follow that the phenomenon does not exist. In other words, while the qualitative dimension of existence may be conveniently dismissed from an exclusively materialistic perspective towards life, nevertheless, experientially, we are entirely familiar with its authenticity and pertinence.

Furthermore, while subjectivity reveals the inadequacy of the feeling nature to provide definitive knowledge, it, nevertheless, demonstrates that an exclusively materialistic point of view is too narrow.

Indeed, it behooves the openminded researcher to pursue the implication of the existence of physically elusive significances because therein an entire volume of meaningfulness is brought to light.

It is readily possible, therefore, that the marginalized qualitative dimension of phenomena is, in reality, of considerable value and even of essential significance. But while qualities and values cannot be quantified for the practical convenience of intellectual justification, nevertheless, the exclusion of intangible evidence engenders a considerable misunderstanding towards existence.

It is obviously true that subjectivity is inconsistent in its evaluation and, upon that basis, materialistic, Western Philosophy appraises existence primarily upon the strength of tangible evidence. But while the evaluation of intangible qualities, values and essential identities will always be subjective when left to human feeling-sentience, our idiosyncratic evaluation is not the exclusive means whereby intangible significances are recognized.

In fact, it does not really matter if we each evaluate physically elusive circumstances differently. However, it is important that we acknowledge their existence because otherwise we are deceived into believing that life is only superficial. Be that as it may, in terms of definite knowledge, the essential singularity, as the authentic, human distinction, possesses the inherent capacity of immediate engagement, and thereby an objective mind can correctly discern intangible significances.

Immediate cognition is possible because the human ipseity resides within the same condition as the qualitative, intangible quintessence of phenomena and, consequently, it is able to discover things in their intrinsic condition of existence. Therefore, we do not need to evaluate, speculate or hypothesize concerning the essential identity of things in material terms because we can recognize them in the condition in which they definitively exist.

In summation, the human, essential singularity is able to engage phenomena immediately, without the potential distraction of the indirect, or subjective, cognitive faculties. Furthermore, the human essence experiences circumstances through direct encounter, eluding the customary, oblique practices of evaluation and intellectual analysis. Thereby, it discovers things originally, in terms of their unique and particular significance.

3. Human Significance

Immediate, experiential engagement enables the human being to discover the intrinsic significance and the particular distinction of the identity of a phenomenon. But this practice should not be confused with heightened, but otherwise conventional, observation, nor with subjective cognition through our feeling-sentient nature. Prerequisite and imperative to direct cognition is the experiential recognition of our own individual, essential existence. Once recognized, our authentic and singular identity must then become established as the seat and cognitive perspective of the observation, in order that the inherent significance of phenomena may be subsequently discovered.

The difficulty in understanding the practice of immediate cognition pertains to the recognition of the human individual ipseity because with increasing resignation Western philosophy denies the existence of all but biological idiosyncrasy. In all likelihood, it probably matters little whether we are convinced of the essential permanency of the intrinsic individual or subscribe to the belief of temporal organic identity. Indeed, although each perspective suggests contradictory psychological ramifications, the practice of immediate cognition answers the question definitively.

The crux of the practice of immediate engagement concerns the restraint of a standard cognitive approach that has become second nature and habitual. Thereby, at least for the duration of our observation, we curb the usual tendencies of feeling-sentient evaluation, partiality and intellectual deliberation. Subsequently, we find that we have established an unimpeded view whereupon all things appear in their essential fullness.

In fact, all at once, when the familiar thinking and interpretive activities are curbed there remains nothing to inhibit direct engagement, and an explicit view becomes readily attainable. Furthermore, if we turn our attention away from the object of observation, but towards ourselves, we discover our own intrinsic selfhood. This occurs because inherently pertaining to the human essential identity is the capacity to experience the similarly elemental existence of all other phenomena, including the significance of itself.

Consequently, through immediate, experiential engagement we recognize the original existence of ourselves, others and all phenomenal appearances. However, we may not be readily capable of appropriately articulating the nature of the intrinsic distinction of a phenomenon because qualitative significances require metaphoric and descriptive versatility, alike to an artistic medium, in order to be communicated. Nevertheless, experientially, through immediate engagement, the essential significance of the human being is thoroughly aware of the elemental and inherent distinction of a thing and recognizes it with the same profundity with which it views its own authentic identity.

Thus, the essential significance of the human constitution is not the superficial appearance nor the corporeal functions, and iIt does not reside in the brain, the heart or in the personality. If it did, it would not possess the capacity to discern the intrinsic significance of things because corporeal functions are incommensurable with existential conditions.

Existential significances are the continuous qualifications of phenomenal identity. They are the way things are in essence. However neither cerebral functions nor emotional evaluation can directly engage the intrinsic circumstances of things because both approaches are indirect and circuitous. Substantive conditions are only experientially discerned through immediate engagement by the human, essential identity. Furthermore, direct cognition occurs instantaneously while reason is a remote process distanced from the actual event in terms of both time and space. Similarly, emotional evaluation and preference while seemingly direct, remain subjective and essentially moot where definitive, existential knowledge is concerned.

However, subjective cognition can be improved towards more precise articulation through training. Indeed, the artistic perspective correctly recognizes that the dimension with which it is preoccupied remains inaccessible to rationale, and endeavors to express it through an alternative medium. This is because qualitative significances, that are the content of artistic communication, must be directly experienced in order to be known.

However, a reasoned interpretation of existence occurs indirectly within the remote domain of the intellect. Indeed, something can be rationalized exhaustively without ever being experienced. Consequently, the evident conflict between abstract explanation and experientially derived knowledge rests upon two distinctly different approaches. That is to say, quantitatively intelligible information concerning phenomena is ideally suited to intellectual functioning because it can be physically justified as extant, and a philosophical argument may be successfully established upon its mathematical representation.

But the qualitative, intangible merit that epitomizes the intrinsic significance of a phenomenon must be directly experienced in order to be recognized. Consequently, intangible values are not successfully transposed into a compatible, accountable condition whereby they can be evaluated in the manner of physical properties. Also, as we know from personal experience, quality cannot be physically distinguished or numerically represented with adequate justice. That is why the intrinsic significance of a phenomenon remains beyond the orbit of an exclusively materialistic perspective.

In real life, the human being constantly evaluates phenomena and circumstances using both approaches.

But the narrow view of materialistic, Western philosophy is established almost exclusively upon the analysis and evaluation of physically derived intelligence. Consequently, the materialistic point of view necessarily minimizes the significance of the essential dimension because intrinsic distinction cannot be assessed in physical terms, and in this connection the substantive cannot be tangibly verified as authentic. That is to say, the existence of physical phenomena is sanctioned upon the basis of material substantiality and corroborated by the measure of the quantifiable properties. However, an exclusively materialistic methodology cannot readily demonstrate the existence of intangible values because they are of a more profound nature than the corporeal, and their validation seems to be only subjectively apparent.

Data that is compatible with an exclusively materialistic perspective must be physically authenticated in order to be assimilable, otherwise it contradicts systematic and sequential logic. Nevertheless, in reality there is no such thing as an exceptional, materialistic philosophy because even the most determined proponent would need to deny the explicit evidence of everyday experience to the contrary. Indeed, ordinary speech is copious with descriptive terminology that qualifies the physically elusive dimension.

However, if an intangible value cannot be demonstrated as extant except through a specious

21

conviction concerning its authenticity, then it must be excluded from consideration. That is to say, if something is acknowledged as extant through experience but otherwise remains physically uncertain, then it becomes extremely difficult to allocate equal significance to the intangible quality when, in comparison, physical properties remain readily and overwhelmingly verifiable.

Materialistic philosophy is therefore at odds with our ordinary life experience because it necessarily excludes the intangible significances that we experientially know to exist and which we find to be of considerable, human significance. Therefore, either the qualitative dimension of existence is of negligible consequence, or the exclusively materialistic interpretation of life, as a philosophical perspective, is profoundly at fault.

4. Feeling Sentience

While the human, feeling nature may readily recognize the qualitative dimension of existence we should not assume that feeling-sentience possesses sufficient competence to definitively distinguish and authenticate between qualitative experiences. That is, the subjective nature of sentiment and sympathy prevents the human emotional nature from conclusive evaluation. However, it is remarkable that only the terse terms of mathematics can successfully represents an isolated physical event without resort to figurative description or anthropomorphic characterization because phenomenal entireties cannot be adequately represented through physics alone.

In other words, a figurative appraisal of existence is not unique to lay people but even the scientist is sometimes tempted by metaphor and allusion. Consequently, by implication, existence does not appear to be adequately described in solely physical terms but must rely upon a qualitative descriptor for the sake of clarity. Indeed, in order to establish a relevant correspondence with reality, terminology pertaining merely to the physical circumstances of things is inadequate in extent.

Nevertheless, felling-sentience is notoriously capricious and consequently it fails to offer a reasonable alternative interpretation of existence. Indeed, the undependable explanation of physically elusive circumstances remains noticeably prevalent among religious devotees but also modern artists of all media. Even so, the emotional interpretation of things is imagined to offer an alternative dimensionality to materialism, and it is expected that feelings somehow acknowledge what the intellect cannot assimilate. In fact, while the feeling-sentient nature may reveal and engage qualitative value, it can never definitively identify intrinsic significances because sentiment is always biased and, consequently, its estimations are inevitably unreliable.

This is particularly pertinent when an intangible value otherwise possesses no physical representation at all. Then, all manner of extraordinary interpretations are possible, some of which bear little resemblance to reality.

But the intellect is equally capable of obscure conclusions. When dialectic exclusively pursues an interpretation of existence founded upon a specialization such as physics, mechanics or electricity, the results are frequently presented as if the physical or electrical aspects and properties of a phenomenon were the exclusive extent. It is imagined that the entirety can be explained in terms of certain specific and isolated attributes, that in fact, merely represent only selected aspects of the whole.

Nevertheless, despite an excessively narrow view, philosophical constructs are established to explain a phenomenon from the perspective of a certain feature as if the facet somehow explained the entirety. Thus, the physical or mathematical approach that is concerned merely with the quantifiable aspects of a phenomenon, may become hypothetically extrapolated and an entire hypothesis accordingly constructed. Alarmingly, abstract scholarship may be assumed to be factual not upon the basis of definitive justification, but through peer consensus.

This is particularly interesting in terms of the application of a theoretical projection because abstract generalization is a human failing that is widely identifiable. Indeed, one hypothesis is sometimes argued against a different theoretical presumption as if the one speculation might somehow definitively disprove an alternative conjecture.

Consequently, it is most important in terms of metaphysics that the understanding of the researcher is securely established upon indisputable evidence. Hence, if we desire to discover the intrinsic distinction of a phenomenon, we concentrate on something that is substantial and avoid the pursuit of unfounded eventualities. For example, the consideration of objects passing at light-speed from the perspective of the passenger holding a timepiece, is as ethereal as esoteric speculation concerning the supernatural power of human volition. Indeed, if we restrain reverie and observe light itself or human wishful fiction in action, we discover a greater profundity. That is to say, the basis of our thinking must consist of something substantial, impartially tested and found reliable in practice, or once more we abandon reality for fabrication and thereby waste much time.

For this reason, while sentiment and intuition may suggest the existence of the qualitative dimension of things, it is the human, essential identity that engages phenomena immediately and discovers their crucial significance. That is to say, the intrinsic human being is able to discern the essential significance of physically conspicuous phenomena through immediate cognition.

Sadly, a prevalent conviction among modern artists insists that one can only grasp the qualitative significance of circumstances, through the feelings. It is believed that a direct encounter by the feelings is of comparative cognitional value to reason. Thereby, it is thought that if the feelings encounter a phenomenon something significant may be precisely identified. But all that is represented is the artist's feelings towards something. That depiction seldom reveals the identity or intrinsic condition of the illusive relevance of a phenomenon.

Artists of this caliber and those philosophically opposed to materialism, maintain that intellectualism is superseded by emotionally driven, heightened awareness because they believe that knowledge is attainable through the scrutiny of a sentimental response to a phenomenon. The materialist meanwhile, marginalizes such self-indulgence as justifiably unreliable but, thereby, the implication of possible elusive, intrinsic significance is similarly overlooked. Consequently, the conflict between the intellectual approach towards life founded upon the physical appearance of things, and the experiential method, remains unresolved because indeed, the feelings do not definitively distinguish the intrinsic identity of things but only suggest their existence. Therefore, it appears as if the qualitative dimension of existence cannot be justified as definitively extant and may be only obliquely acknowledged through subjective experience. But this is not the case.

If we engage something originally, as if for the first time, from the perspective of our human, intrinsic identity, a considerable volume of significance becomes apparent. We restrain our intellect because we do not wish to interpret a situation through rationale, and similarly, we observe impartially without sentiment because we wish to discover the inherent identity of the object straightforwardly. Thereby, we avoid preconceived expectation that may confuse and interfere, and approach the circumstances of our investigation with impeccable ingenuousness.

From this description we recognize a corresponding approach between immediate cognition, and the practice of openhearted sincerity outlined in the first chapter. In terms of immediate cognition, with the objective of discovering the essential significances that underlies the obvious appearance of things, a necessary clarity of perspective should not be disrupted by predisposed evaluation and anticipation. Indeed, in order to faithfully discern the intrinsic nature of the existence of a phenomenon the attentive receptivity of an open mind is essential.

5. Immediate Experience

Through the straightforward experience of immediate cognition, we recognize the unsatisfactory nature of a philosophical interpretation of existence that is established remotely from actual circumstances and we realize that we do not in fact require an explanation at all. That is to say, by virtue of a direct unaffected approach we discover the way things actually exist of themselves.

In the same vein, the significant identity of the human being is not revealed through indirect, intellectual evaluation nor properly identified by means of the feeling nature. Neither do the materialistic sciences possess the necessary range to pinpoint the human quintessence. Nevertheless, the individual ipseity discovers itself through direct experiential engagement.

However, the immediate experience of the human, essential existence is not of vital significance to the practice of direct cognition. That is to say, upon the restraint of the faculties of indirect evaluation, the human essential significance of necessity comes to the forefront. But the ipseity cannot be verified as authentic either through abstract computation or by the feelings, yet it is discovered experientially when those appraising activities are inhibited. That is, the human, individual ipseity experiences itself directly, as an intangible identity and from that perspective it discerns the existential significance of all things including itself. Thereby, we find that we are not a corporeal function or a biological anomaly but a unique existence.

For this reason, the discovery of the human, intrinsic relevance is not contingent upon mental sophistication, nor upon an inconstant feeling nature. But, in order that the essential can be revealed and verified, the human, individual singularity must become established as the primary perspective. Thus, we accomplish immediacy by the restraint of oblique, indirect estimation. Thereby, the ipseity is demonstrated as extant through self-recognition and further substantiated by a cognitive supremacy over the conventional faculties of reason and feeling evaluation. Indeed, that which exerts an influence over the cerebral faculties and restrains feeling-sentient evaluation, is inevitably our own authentic identity. Thus, the human, essential significance is found to exist in a state of immediate relevance as the ultimate authority of the human constitution.

Furthermore, it is from the perspective of our essential identity that we are able to discover the intrinsic significance of other people, and of all phenomena. We readily achieve this because the ipseity exists essentially in a condition of immediacy, where only imminent reality is of pertinence. In other words, we discover the similarly significant, essential existence of other phenomena because intrinsically we inhabit the same existential circumstances.

However, materialistic, Western philosophy is

founded upon systematic argument wherein, ideally, every premise is sequentially justified. But physical exclusivity requires that nothing should be included towards a logical construct that cannot be demonstrated as materially authentic. Nevertheless, the essential significances that we discern through direct cognition are intangible, and consequently, a philosophy that dismisses the profound volume that underlies the appearance of things, will be inevitably insufficient.

This is the status quo of materialistic Western philosophy; it necessarily learns heavily upon physical evidence because tangibility is the integral premise of its foundation. Meanwhile, the intangible, qualitative dimension of existence is neglected because it can only be experientially qualified as authentic. Thus, qualities and intrinsic significance that are empirically known to exist, cannot be included in the equation because their importance is unjustifiable compared to the manner whereby the physical is easily recognized and quantified.

The challenge is not whether the qualitative dimension of a phenomenon is real, but how its significance can be included while it remains physically elusive. Indeed, qualities are universally accepted, but the shortcomings of the intellect, as the supposed, final arbiter of accounts, prevent their philosophical inclusion thereby reducing our view of existence to the shallow, quantifiable, physical components.

We find ourselves in this impasse because we are

ignorant of the inherent capacity of our own essential identity to recognize the intrinsic, intangible significance of phenomena. Furthermore, humanity has a confused history of irrational credulity, and no one wants a return of preternatural superstition. Nevertheless, the qualitative significances of things are found to possess far greater importance in terms of the identity of a phenomenon than their physical counterparts, which are discovered to be comparatively, merely superficial.

Unfortunately, a strictly materialistic philosophical approach is such that the reality of a human, essential identity, that exists incorporeally, is no more acceptable or rational than that which the human feelings insist is relevant, but remain unable to conclusively justify. We must therefore conclude, that the intellectual approach towards existence is inadequate in terms of definitive identification. Fortunately, we do not need to rely on reason or sentiment in order to discover the authenticity of essential but intangible significances; nor in order to recognize the inherent, cognitive autonomy of the individual, human essence.

The qualitative dimension of existence cannot be simply dismissed because it fails to correspond with physically established standards, but the greater profundity that we directly experience must be understood as the expository qualifier of the existential significance of phenomena. Therein lies the meaning of the physical carapace that otherwise makes little sense without it.

In other words, the human, feeling-sentient nature reveals the existence of the qualitative, but our cerebral processes cannot logically manage capricious information. But a quality does not possess physical substance nor can it be proven to exist or be represented in physical terms, but that does not disqualify its existence. Thus, the qualitative significance of a phenomenon is real and remains experientially recognized as authentic, even though intangible values cannot be justified and exactly calibrated through quantification in the manner as physical objects.

However, the summary disqualification of qualitative information through an exclusively materialistic philosophy is not merely derived from the inconsistency of interpretation provided through our feeling nature. But the qualitative significance of something is of a constitution that is incommensurate with the manner whereby the physical appearance is acknowledged and simply cannot be assessed in the same way as material substance because of its intangibility.

But the materialist is afraid that if intangible evidence is ceded the same significance as the physical, then we will lose our orientation and fantasy will replace fact as the acceptable standard. Indeed, there is considerable justification in this conviction. However, upon the practice of immediate cognition intangible significances no longer remain vague impressions but become definitive, expressive forces.

However, the existence of qualitative value is begrudgingly acquiesced because it must be. But through partial and representative quantification, significance is inevitably all but abandoned from our materialistically biased understanding of life. Unfortunately, the disqualification of the philosophical pertinence of the qualitative dimension of existence, by the same measure, also rejects experiential knowledge concerning our own intangible, individual identity. They are imagined to be similarly illusive peculiarities of subjective interpretation.

Indeed, the attribution of human, intrinsic significance merely to the physical body is a grave presumption beyond mere philosophical differences. Thereby, the possibility of immediate cognition is effectively banished because the perspective of the ipseity is indispensable. Indeed, it is the ipseity that transforms subjective experience into definitive knowledge.

As we have already stated, the exclusively materialistic approach requires that the intangible be presented in a physical form in order that it may be authenticated, but the qualitative existence of something cannot be materially confined. The materialist, therefore, renders the human, individual identity into physical and logically demonstrable terms, establishing its existence, tangibly. Thereby, it reduces the significance of the human, essential distinction by elevating the status of a convenient corporeal organ wherein the human identity might be fittingly accommodated. Thus, the human, singularity of existence and sovereign identity are replaced by the physical brain.

Through this legerdemain, the human identity is reduced in consequence to a property of the transient body. Thereby, the significance of our human, essential existence that is capable of directly determining the intrinsic identity of phenomena, is negated. Thus, the human essence that endures as an eternal and incorporeal existence in a condition of immediacy, is replaced with a physical counterfeit that is existentially meaningless.

Consequently, the human, feeling sentience is elevated as the sole witness of intangible existence. Thereby, it endeavors to determine the authentic nature and identity of something otherwise elusive but fails us in terms of definitive knowledge, through subjective interpretation. Therefore, our feeling capacity misinterprets the intangible significances of phenomena through its unavoidably credulous and inconstant assessment. Indeed, how we feel about something or what we feel something to be is mostly irrelevant in terms of conclusive identification. The feelings are unable to provide intrinsic and existential knowledge, strongly influenced as they are by predisposition and preference.

In other words, sentiment cannot offer conclusive

evidence and, consequently, it distracts from the immediate engagement of the essential existence of a thing. Consequently, feeling-sentience along with rationale and partiality must be restrained in order that the human, essential distinction may directly and originally engage circumstances.

Thus, subjectively derived information, founded upon suspicion and nuances of feeling is qualitatively polar opposite to the materialistic stance and that is why materialistic Western philosophy cannot include it in a conventional world-view. The materialist, consequently discards intangible evidence altogether, convinced that the physical aspects alone offer conclusive knowledge.

But reason is similarly inadequate in terms of discovering the intrinsic existence of something because it cannot experience or approach a phenomenon immediately. Indeed, the advocate for materialistic, Western philosophy is persuaded by exhaustively reasoned dialectic, founded exclusively upon physical evidence, that the intellect alone is capable of determining the nature of a phenomenon. Paradoxically, in contradiction, those convinced of the infallibility of feeling-sentience, refute the very same exclusive materialism on the basis of their own enigmatic and inexplicable explanations.

However, both approaches fail us. The intellect must pursue every line of reasoning and consider a situation from all perspectives, yet it always remains inadequate in terms of definitive, existential knowledge because of the indirectness of its operation. Similarly, the human, feeling-sentient nature is personal and can never present conclusive evidence concerning the authentic nature of things. Thus, both practices are misappropriated when it comes to the determination of the intrinsic identity and qualitative significance of something. They are mutually incompatible, and each provides only partial knowledge while both remain constitutionally incapable of achieving definitive, profound understanding.

Yet, the one as well as the other, champion the reliability of their perspective. Accordingly, it is evident that both practices must involve a level of unfounded belief and biased conviction because neither offer conclusive resolution. Ideally, a caveat expressing the limitations of the particular, cognitive practice would need to append to all apparent discoveries that extend beyond the conspicuous limits of the approach. Thereby, reservations concerning the value of subsequent philosophical conclusions would, accordingly, be openly acknowledged.

Unfortunately, we do not always recognize or select strict integrity over conviction and, consequently, we find that the defense of an embattled position achieves precedence over stringent impartiality.

Nevertheless, reality is not a state exclusively established upon physical circumstances, and it is a small portrayal indeed that assumes otherwise. Anything less than the most profound understanding fails to approach the way things actually are, and, comparatively, appears as a hollow philosophy or an elaborate belief, remote from reality. Yet, the moment that we encounter something directly from the perspective of our intrinsic existence, we engage phenomena as they fundamentally and essentially exist and not as we reason or imagine them to be. Thereupon, no further cognitive necessity beyond the discovery of the intrinsic significance and existential condition of a phenomenon is required.

Nevertheless, untried, cognitive immediacy seems to represent an unnecessary approach to understanding compared with accustomed rationale because the intellect evaluates at a certain distance and the long perspective suggests objectivity. Indeed, reflection is the confident methodology and with the evidence of acumen and established intelligence there appears to exist a sufficiently reliable triad.

Unfortunately, partial, exclusive physically derived information of a selected calibre inevitably results in a similarly superficial conclusion, that in this case is represented by a banal materialistic philosophy. Fortunately, the intrinsic existence of the human being possesses the capacity to identify a substantive volume that is only implied by the physical circumstances, and otherwise remains elusive. The skeptic will question concerning the location because only the three dimensions of material existence are acknowledged. But through straightforward, openminded cognition we discern an immanent, indwelling volume wherein the essential significances of all things reside. Furthermore, the immediate engagement of physical circumstances and the direct experience of the profound and meaningful essence of things answers those countless questions that remain perplexing from an exclusively material perspective.

Belief systems and revelations, even from the most trusted source, pale in comparison to our own immediate encounter with imminent circumstances. Furthermore, we are dissatisfied with someone else's considered assessments or hypothetical constructs that purport to explain existence. For that reason, nothing compares with intelligence derived through the direct engagement of phenomena by our own innate singularity because the human, incorporeal ipseity inhabits an impendent condition, wherein everything is revealed in its intrinsic state through the immediate manner of an encounter.

40

6. Incorporeal Existence

While it is certainly accurate to say that immediate cognition profoundly impresses the human mind leading to a more meaningful perspective towards life, nevertheless, a tenacious, dysfunctional mentality is not necessarily liberated without considerable difficulty. Indeed, there may not appear to be any particular dispositional improvement in spite of insightful understanding.

The reason for this concerns the existentially intense, confirmed conditioning that indoctrinates the human soul according to an idiosyncratic inclination. In this regard, it is as if an established dispositional paradigm predominated the human psyche based upon an inflexible self-perpetuating design.

Consequently, the human mind must be impacted more deeply than the level of occasional discernment or the acquisition of knowledge. Required is an overwhelming independent force that can move the heart-of-the-soul wherein the increasingly moribund mentality was first conceived. In other words, it is as if we had each become habituated according to diverse, dispositional propensities that subordinate a worthier potential. It is this situation that must be overcome in order that human existence may become more consciously substantive.

For this reason, the construction of a humanly

contrived ethos is too superficial to address the development of a successive nature that can carry the individual towards a meaningful future. Furthermore, while the experience of essential existence provides a respite from the turbidity of a dysfunctional mind, unfortunately immediate cognition also fails us because perception and comprehension do not sufficiently impress the predetermined heart.

Inevitably, the mentality that originated and was further developed within the psyche must be remedied through a similar process. Indeed, upon even a most cursory reflection we recognize that the inclination of the heart was pivotal to the establishment of our present disposition for both right or wrong.

In other words, predilections arise from the nature of the respective soul that pursued from birth a particular dispositional affinity, and further crafted a characteristic demeanor through reiteration or change of heart. Consequently, desiring the establishment of an ethos that is appropriate to a substantive future and a qualitatively worthwhile succeeding development, dispositional reorientation is imperative. In other words, humanity requires an appropriate integrity befitting a significant destiny.

Through the practice of immediate cognition, we recognize that the material appearance is an unrepresentative portion of the full existence of things. Consequently, it is of no surprise that the exemplary principle of a successive human disposition is also immanently essential and must be engaged through similar straightforwardness.

Perhaps it is unfortunate that we must leave the certain physical parameters to which we are accustomed and endeavor to pursue the emancipation of a moribund mentality, seemingly without navigational bearings. Nevertheless, in reality, we do in fact retain a sound orientation when we embark upon dispositional improvement as we did when we anchored our attention to the physical semblance in order to discern the essential significance of the material.

That is to say, in order to recognize the authentic identity of a phenomenon, we discovered the necessity of distinguishing the qualitative nature of its expression from the obvious appearance. Thereby, we found that everything possesses an innate statement of existence that is the intrinsic constitutional identity. Furthermore, if we remain preoccupied with only the mechanics and artificers of a thing we overlook the existential significance and fail to grasp the implication that the discovery of essential identity presents. Thereby, we remain oblivious to the dimension of existence that is comprised not merely of physical conditions, but intrinsic significance and essential identity. Inevitably, our narrow view remains wanting.

In a similar superficial manner, we can try to analyze the existing human mentality and determine to balance the advantages and shortcomings of a particular mentality indefinitely. However, without the standard of a separate exemplary principle we cannot successfully refashion the human psyche.

Fortunately, the sound navigational bearings earlier intimated resemble those of immediate cognition in principle although not in form. In the case of dispositional amelioration, certainty is discovered through openhearted sincerity. That is to say, the unimpeded heart, as the formative locus of the human character, also serves us as a direct and absolute conduit between the individual and the supernal nature.

With reference once more to immediate cognition, the intrinsic significance and essential identity of something portend to an otherwise intangible dimension of existence that is composed of substantive relevance. In other words, essential conditions are known through the qualitative statement of their existence. Consequently, in order to discern the intrinsic distinction of things the observer must attend to the quintessential, characteristic nature that qualitatively epitomizes what they are.

It is the same with openhearted sincerity. Through ingenuousness the heart establishes an affinity with an extrinsic, sound mind that resides immanently and contiguously, and is approached by an open conscience. That is to say, the heart is the optimum approach between the psyche and an exemplary disposition in the same manner as the ipseity accomplishes immediate cognition. Consequently, immediacy unimpeded by sentimental distraction anticipates a pristine communion.

For example, the intrinsic significance of a material phenomenon is the incorporeal justification. Thus, the identity is only superficially physical, but the inherent expressional motif of the existence of a thing is the more profound particularity. However, intrinsic identity is only discerned experientially and cannot be adequately described merely through a scrutiny of the physical evidence. Consequently, we discover the intrinsic significance of things, not superficiality but through insight.

The parallel with openhearted sincerity is conspicuous. That is to say, we cannot specify the supernal nature in physical terms any more that we can describe essential significances dimensionally. Likewise, the exemplary nature that we experience through a receptive heart is discerned experientially within the most profound substance of the human constitution. Nevertheless, the straightforward approach may be confused in the same way by sentimentality in a manner that resembles more closely, preconceptual distraction. In that sense, we recognize that directly ascertained knowledge is vastly more viable than any indirect rational supposition concerning it. What is more, we cannot clarify the existence of the exemplary principle that we discover within the heart through further exposition, nevertheless, it is known personally without a shadow of doubt through openhearted sincerity.

Accordingly, we find that the essential distinction of something is the substantive and meaningful integrity of its existence, and significance resides independently of an assessment of the appearance, yet it underlies the focal representation. Thus, the physical appearance coordinates the attention of the observer, and when the material condition is immediately engaged by the essential human being, the intrinsic distinction of the object is revealed.

In other words, in order to discover the inherent nature of the existence of something, it must be engaged not cursorily, but immediately from an acute perspective. But while the most profound point of view possible is that of the human, intrinsic distinction, the qualitative timbre of the heart determines human integrity. Consequently, a redundant mentality is successfully superseded when through sincerity we permit the supernal to reestablish the nature of the human psyche according to a successive paradigm.

Indeed, unfeigned contrition is the proper relationship towards the supernal nature because we know full well that the former mentality has failed us miserably, and the future remains unknown. That is to say, open conscience allows the inauguration of a successive disposition in preference to a dishonest continued justification of our deficiencies and misconduct.

Both the approach of immediate cognition and of

openhearted sincerity towards the immanent supernal nature, are remarkable through the necessity of individual straightforwardness. Gone is the mystery of the specially gifted clairvoyant and the intuitive soothsayer. Henceforth, we cannot be misled by fanciful divination or an elite ecclesiastical authority if we engage circumstances plainly for ourselves. Indeed, personally accrued knowledge of this calibre serves as a benchmark of authenticity that vastly supersedes the conjecture of revelatory premonition.

Thus, immediate engagement through the individual singularity of existence enables us to discover the elemental condition of things to the degree that we discontinue conventional appraisal. However, the insight that arises inevitably concerns essential significances of already apparent physical conditions. Conversely, the drifting imagination of the psychic deals with how the practitioner feels about something and not the intrinsic significance of phenomena. For this reason, it is not enough to restrain our thinking and associative practices. Of comparable importance, instinctual, feeling interpretation must also be discontinued in order to avoid make-believe.

Hence, through openhearted sincerity the emphasis is upon honesty and ingenuousness whereby nothing is allowed to mediate between ourselves and the immanent exemplar.

Direct apprehension allows a phenomenon to be

experience as it is within the state of its intrinsic and essential existence. Thus, the original engagement of phenomena, and of their inherent circumstances, without the intrusion of our own emotional interpretation or intellectual appraisal, is the manner whereby something is discovered as it exists intrinsically. Thereby, we discern the qualitative nature of its expression and, consequently, the essential significance that is the characteristic nomen.

Everything possesses intrinsic significance. We can either navigate through life only remotely aware and peripherally engaged, or become steadily cognizant of a vast, overlooked meaningful proportion that epitomizes the essential implication. In other words, be become alert to integral relevance as opposed to the superficial view and thereby life becomes substantive, purposeful and literal.

That is to say, the intrinsic condition of a thing is engaged and discerned when the essential significance of the human being confronts an object straightforwardly, so that the individual selfhood meets the phenomenon directly. This is possible because the human ipseity is fundamental and, consequently, it can immediately recognize authenticity because it resides within the same state wherein the profound condition of everything is discerned.

Furthermore, all intangible significances exist imminently, without spatial and cognitive dissociation. But, the immanent volume wherein the substantive significance of phenomena resides, is not another place. Indeed, in the same way that the superficial perspective presents an alternative perception, essential existence is entirely and immediately present. Consequently, we recognize that the shallow view is the fault of human insensibility and ignorance because it concerns a dullness of discernment and not the discovery of an alternative location.

It is entirely the same with respect to openhearted sincerity and the reorientation of the human psyche. In order that the moribund mentality can be superseded by a worthy disposition, the heart must render itself receptive to supernal influence. This is accomplished by guileless susceptibility. Indeed, we have everything to gain by the unpretentious surrender of an inveterate moribund mentality.

Similarly, it is enormously important in terms of a meaningful future, that conventional cognition through emotional evaluation and preference, or by intellectual appraisal, be superseded by the direct approach from the perspective of the human, essential singularity. The former practices cannot possibly offer definitive knowledge except in the most superficial manner whereby conclusions are formed based upon the merely physical appearance.

Similarly, a redundant mindset that promises only further distress and confusion has become insidiously entrenched and it is this way of thinking and feeling that must be replaced. If we hang on to a certain confidence in a narrow perspective and a petty sense of self, the successive nature cannot become established.

In other words, unless circumstances are directly engaged from the point of view of the human ipseity, the profundity of things cannot be definitively ascertained. And unless the soul renders the heart vulnerable towards the supernal ethos, we remain arrested in a state of inertia.

Thus, neither the shallow superficial view towards existence, nor the moribundity of the petty nature offer a meaningful futurity because they are both obsolete in the light of a swiftly developing consciousness. In this sense, we need to abandon the former mentality and allow a new perspective and an appropriately mature disposition to become established within the human constitution.

The human ipseity is the singular significance of human existence. It is incorporeal and as such it can only be experientially recognized. Consequently, the entire relevance of immediate cognition rests upon the significance of the intrinsic human being.

Similarly, the heart of the soul directly engages the supernal ethos through acceptive sincerity, and thereby alters the qualitative, dispositional timbre of the individual in preparedness for a worthwhile futurity. Indeed, the present human trajectory under the sway of a constricted mindset and unpleasant mien of self-first is unsupported and without meaningful subsequence. In other words, there is no option but the consummation of further qualitative maturation.

The condition in which the essential significance of ourselves, others and phenomena exist, is immediacy. But in terms of the comprehensive view it is also the more profound and significant context. Formerly, we viewed circumstances only peripherally, and even though we reasoned exhaustively concerning existence and assumed that because our thoughts were systematically argued, that we were well informed, the subsequent view remained too narrowly circumscribed. But reality as an existential condition, cannot be known through conceptualization. Therefore, the full volume of existence must be experienced directly in order to be justified. That is to say, the overlooked intrinsic significance of things have to be directly ascertained in order to be known.

Predictably, in terms of the qualitative timbre of the human soul, we discover an obvious parallel. That is, it is impossible to discover the nature of a successive disposition from the perspective of unfamiliarity, but we discern the supernal ethos through the immediate engagement of a receptive heart. Thereby, we no longer confuse obliquely derived conjecture with empirical knowledge.

52

7. The Human Singularity

Awareness of the unique and singular nature of our human identity, and of the intangible significance of phenomena, can occur spontaneously from time to time. A glimpse of essential circumstances may suddenly overwhelm us and take our breath away. This is produced through an impromptu, immediate engagement by the human ipseity sometimes launched by a poignant event. The human, sovereign singularity comes inadvertently to the fore when our conventional faculties are momentarily restrained through the impression of a beautiful vista or something of that nature; similarly awe-inspiring.

However, exposure to the full significance of the existence of things need not be only a capricious experience because, intrinsically, we possess the inherent capacity to directly engage phenomena from the perspective of our authentic existence. That is to say, unhindered by intellectual interpretation, prejudicial conceptualization and emotional evaluation, the human essence naturally encounters circumstances directly, without hindrance.

Immediacy provides an experiential engagement of phenomena in the condition in which things exist meaningfully, in full reality. It is through directness that the human essence is able to apprehend things as they actually are. Thereby, we determine that the human being already, inherently possess a measure of significant, cognitional independence. Consequently, things can be originally and objectively discerned by an appropriately receptive mind, and we do not have to anticipate extraordinary consciousness. In other words, if we can spontaneously experience intrinsic circumstances, it must be inherent within us to intentionally do the same.

It is unnecessary to believe in the cognitive efficacy of immediate cognition or the existence of the human, essential identity, because we can know them definitively for ourselves through personal experience. But it is essential to restrain predispositions because partiality hinders open-minded research. Otherwise, preconceptual bias against the possibility that immediate engagement could be an authentic, perceptual option, or that the human singularity of existence might, indeed be discoverable through direct cognition, narrows our view.

Furthermore, pre-established conviction and preferential bias is particularly damaging when the conclusive demonstration of the existence of the intangible significance of phenomena requires the application of the already dismissed practice. In other words, if we refuse to research the efficacy of an idea because we reject the means whereby it may be appropriately examined, a hypothesis remains permanently conjectural.

That is to say, if an unconventional situation is approached from a cognitive position of established prejudice that excludes unfamiliar evidence, then the researcher is already adversely convinced and need inquire no further. But if circumstances are engaged from a position of open-mindedness and prior evaluation is postponed, inevitably the possibility of a unique discovery remains open. Accordingly, when the conventional cognitive practices are restrained in order that the human singularity of existence may come to the fore in the manner of spontaneous profundity, and an immediate encounter with a phenomenon ensues, things are revealed and verified not notionally but experientially.

A significant pre-conceptual hurdle may concern, not the existence of the human singularity itself, but whether our essential identity possesses the capacity of immediate cognition. In this way we recognize how speculative thinking may prevent direct investigation. In other words, if the possibility of the existence of incorporeal, human singularity is explored experientially and not approached merely as if it were an intellectual concept to be evaluated, our concerns are groundless. Thus, the significance of the human singularity of existence, upon which direct cognition depends, is not definitively verifiable through rationale. Moreover, an existential condition must be experienced in order to be evaluated, or it otherwise remains indeterminate.

An abstractly established point of view cannot offer definitive knowledge because of the indirect manner in which the intellect functions. Abstraction does not involve immediacy but evaluates situations remotely upon the strength of available information. But there is little definitive intelligence possible concerning physically elusive conditions and consequently they must be tried in practice. Otherwise, the merit of a proposition may be agued indefinitely, but a conclusive resolution can never be attained except through empirical evaluation.

This may seem to imply that immediate cognition involves subjective appraisal and, indeed, this would be the case if the feeling-sentience of the human being were involved. But cognition through immediate experience, as we have described, is not evaluative but involves direct acquaintance. Indeed, intellectual, abstract assessment is considerably more prone to subjectivity because information is manipulated and negotiated in the absence of the phenomenon. Consequently, the existence of something may be well argued through logic but the resultant conclusions, nevertheless, remain unsupported in reality. However, immediate engagement, from the perspective of the human, singularity of existence, avoids subjective evaluation because it involves directly ascertained knowledge without the intrusion of intermediary interpretation.

Respective, essential existence is the authentic, human identity, and it is the unique, singular distinction that intrinsically differentiates one person from another. It is indeed a very strange thing that while this is known experientially by everyone, nevertheless, an extraordinary philosophy has arisen and become significantly accepted, that equates individuality exclusively with the body.

Thereby, directly ascertained knowledge concerning the actual person is eclipsed through the abstract conviction that intellectual and emotional calculation somehow possesses precedence.

Nevertheless, as we have already explored, corporeal faculties cannot directly experience; only a human entity can immediately engage a situation. In other words, thinking is an indirect function which is why the intellect cannot conclusively evaluate unless it calculates information upon mathematical metrics.

Further, it is presumed through remote thinking and oblique appraisal, that notional assessment has superior authority over immediate discernment. But abstract deliberation and estimation are indirect practices that occur distantly from the actual phenomenon. Indeed, the object or situation of interest is only indirectly considered, and the intrinsic significance of a thing can never be discovered if we are convinced that the removed, evaluative approach is unrivaled. Thereby, we distill abstracted information concerning the physical properties of phenomena and ingest them intellectually while abandoning immediate engagement and straightforward experience which would otherwise reveal the way things exist profoundly in their entirety.

The intrinsic significance of something cannot be discovered in any other manner except through immediate engagement. Neither the intellect nor emotional evaluation can reveal authentic existence; they can only portray a conceptional version of it. That is to say, oblique cognitive approaches are incommensurate with experiential knowledge by virtue of the secondary manner in which they operate. Furthermore, originality of perception explicitly requires the unique perspective of the human, essential identity because theorization and inference are managed only approximately and speculatively.

The experience of the condition of immediacy is of greater significance than conventional cognition because directly engaged, everything is found as it exists in immediate actuality. There is no necessity to hypothesize, conjecture or speculate because the phenomenon is discovered in its original condition and recognized by the human, essential identity without intermediation.

It is of no surprise that once phenomena are directly engaged by the human entity itself, that the indirect approach pales beside immediately ascertained knowledge. This occurs because straightforward cognition is an inherent capacity of the human, essential being that itself exists immediately.

Consequently, through original engagement, the human entity becomes aware of the immediate, elemental environment wherein all things are essential and immanent. Thereby, immediate cognition alone allows something to be experienced as it emphatically exists. Indeed, we cannot claim to know what reality is until we engage phenomena fundamentally as they exist in their own right.

For example, if we examine a bird's egg directly from the perspective of our own incorporeal significance, the reality of its elemental significance, independent of our evaluation, is our foremost impression. That is to say, the discovery of the actuality of its existence, demonstrates that we have engaged the circumstance of the phenomenon immediately, and that we have entered the condition of immanence wherein cognition is a direct experience.

Formerly we knew little of the condition of the actual existence of the bird's egg as it pertains to itself. We always just thought about it and endeavored to understand it through information concerning the physical and associative properties. Or we relied on our feeling preferences and evaluated it subjectively. However, now, we discover the bird's egg as it exists in and of itself, irrespective of how we might choose to evaluate it. That is to say, by virtue of the authenticity of our own incorporeal existence we discover further intrinsic significances and we are no longer preoccupied solely with the conclusions of indirect evaluation.

Moreover, as we continue to engage the phenomenon of the bird's egg from the perspective of our own singular existence, we find, through the immediate experience of its existence, that the egg is deliberately established. We discover this through immediate engagement whereby the actual existence of the egg is directly recognized. Thus, it is found to exist as a general conception, yet each species differs in the manner of its realization according to the specific nature of its expression.

We recognize that we failed to see this before because our conventional cognition was always indirect and interpretative, or we were otherwise instructed. But now we are occupied with the phenomenon itself and its intrinsic significance is readily evident through the direct approach. We do not imagine the egg to be anything other than what it is and we have no desire to do so. We engage it immediately and find, not merely a phenomenon possessed of physical properties, but we discover the existence of a general conceptualization that commands a universal application. Thus, we enter the realm of intangible significances through our own singularity of existence and discover the intrinsic origin of things.

Clearly, the single most profitable and significant experiential information that the human being may possess is the immediate cognition of the human, essential existence. Upon this knowledge all other existential intelligence is established. Thereby, the authentic, human identity can no longer be confused with our corporeal constitution because the human essence has been experientially recognized as an entity. Consequently, it is through the perspective of our own essential singularity that a phenomenon, such as a bird's egg, is discovered in the condition of its actual existence.

Intellectually, it is hard to grasp the significance of our own individual existence. That is because it must be immediately experienced and, consequently, established as the perspective from which phenomena are directly and originally engaged. However, this is only achieved without the intrusion of abstract conceptualization and emotional preference. Indeed, they must be restrained or direct engagement is compromised.

Therefore, facing a phenomenon originally without pre-conceptual interpretation and prejudice, the human, essential singularity discovers the intrinsic, elemental significance of the phenomenal appearance. The general concept that dictates the necessity of the bird's egg is invisible and incorporeal, consequently it is not readily assimilable nor intellectually credible. But the analytical approach cannot fathom phenomena that endure without a physical presence because they are unverifiable through conventional cognition. Even though all of its own concepts and ideas reside intangibly in the imagination until physically realized, the materially preoccupied intellect remains unconvinced of the significance of conceptual origins in Nature. Nevertheless, the phenomenal world is inundated with conceptual generalizations that are subsequently realized physically and particularly, although they continues to exist intangibly.

Through immediate cognition the human entity engages phenomena as if for the first time. It is an original and immediate experience that enables us to recognize the emphatically extant significance of things. Yet, the skeptic, preoccupied with an abstract, analytical approach will never discover essential existence because it is supposed that oblique reason is superior to direct engagement. It is assumed that the experiential approach is subjective and varies depending on the individual perspective. Unfortunately, nothing but immediate experience through the aegis of the human singularity of existence can dislodge this counterproductive conviction.

Furthermore, there is a distinction between subjectivity that is founded upon personal preference or prejudiced interpretation, and the direct approach of the human, essential existence. The former is indeed variable and unreliable, established upon feelings and opinions, but the human essence is neither the emotional nature nor the calculative component of the human constitution. In other words, as an entity, the human singularity of existence engages phenomena directly and, consequentially, without precondition. Indeed, there is no direct cognition possible unless all prejudice is postponed because pre-established notions interfere and corrupt the immediate encounter. Thus, the intimate manner whereby the human essence engages phenomena is indeed personal, but it is not subjective because it does not attempt to evaluate; that is to say, it is direct and unbiased.

There exists only one reality, and the immediate approach towards it is the only possible manner of cognition that the human essence recognizes. It is unable to alter the situation because it experiences existence directly as it is. Similarly, the human essence does not evaluate information concerning phenomena in the manner of the intellect or of human feeling-sentience; it merely engages things as they happen to be. Indeed, immediacy precludes the possibility of an impaired and subjective perspective that is variable and inconstant and influenced by preference. Thus, there is only one point of view possible through the direct engagement of the human singularity of existence, and that involves the intrinsic significance of the phenomenon.

Very few people are familiar with immediate, experiential cognition and, consequently, it is a practice that inevitably will be evaluated through the intellect and the emotions based upon selective, individual preconceptions. Unfortunately, the human essence is only discovered through immediate cognition and its existence cannot be justified except through direct experience. However, while we may not recognize the significance of our individual existence, yet we glimpse our uniqueness from time to time. It is therefore, not such an extreme perspective as the philosophical materialist would like to suggest. Indeed, we already have some unspecified and capricious experience of essential circumstances.

In other words, the human, essential ipseity is the authentic identity of the human being and it takes very little effort in order to establish with certainty the existence of our individual uniqueness. That our exclusive singularity exists potentially as the sovereign significance of our constitution and possesses the capacity to discover essential significances directly, is only described with difficulty and inadequately alluded to, but once experienced it is fully justified.

While we constantly discover intangible circumstances through our own, everyday experiences, the qualities and values of things have no significant physical appearance. But materialistic, Western philosophy has established a contrived interpretation of existence wherein everything must be physically verifiable in order to be included and in order to considered significant. Thus, we have granted to the authority of a few through their abstract scholarship, the right to determine that which constitutes existential authenticity. And they have determined that only the physical is real. They have decreed that material substantiality is alone pertinent to an understanding of existence, while the contrary experience of the qualitative, intrinsic dimension of life reveals the opposite. Thereby, the legerdemain of the materialist has dulled our own appreciation of the intangible nature of existence.

Nevertheless, even though qualities are not

tangibly represented they cannot be seriously denied, however the materialistic philosopher degrades their significance and reduces them to the status of a mere adjunct of the physical. Thus, preoccupied with the appearance, it is imagined that the entirety of existence is materially established while the substantive dimension is conveniently marginalized as by the by.

Be that as it may, while intangible significances are physically illusive, they qualify the physical appearance of a phenomenon with meaning. Thus, the challenge to materialistic, Western philosophy is successfully made through the reintroduction of existential significance to the qualitative dimension of phenomena, and the experiential manner in which intangible values are directly recognized.

Only a very distorted and entirely abstract perspective could seriously deny intangible qualities and values. Nevertheless, the materialist lives one thing and espouses an alternative philosophy, summarily dismissing the direct approach whereby essential significances are discovered, even without further inquiry. They fear that if the relevance of intrinsic existence is philosophically reintroduced, then the entire physically established exclusivity of the materialistic approach will be found wanting. Nevertheless, if the qualitative dimension of existence is denied then materialistic, Western philosophy goes against converse, common experience. Its foundational premise is, thereby, disputed and it is recognized that the entire edifice is merely theoretical and abstract, established upon a very distinct, entirely materialistic prejudice.

Through the recognition of the significance of the marginalized qualitative dimension of phenomenal existence, we acknowledge that intangible values are only successfully authenticated, through immediate engagement. It is a small step from there to restrain our conventional practices of cognition and turn our attention to our own individual uniqueness. Thereupon, we recognize that the immediate discovery of the incorporeal significance of the human singularity of existence is the agency whereby human cognition attains autonomy. And from the perspective of our singular existence, we discern the intrinsic significance of others and of all phenomena, and thereby we find that we can engage everything in the condition in which they emphatically and meaningfully exist.

8. Unique Identity

The incorporeal nature of the unique singularity of the human being is evident through self-recognition. This is not a belief nor a dogmatic conviction, but it is experientially derived knowledge concerning the condition of our existence. We encounter our individual significance through immediate cognition whereupon we discern that the individual ipseity is an enduring entity, without material necessity.

Immediate engagement through the aegis of the human, singularity of existence, reveals the meaningful, intangible dimension of the physical appearance of a thing. Conventionally, phenomena are only attributed material significance as the entirety of the substance. But we have now explored the merit of the qualitative value of things, that is normally not considered important to its existence. Consequently, we discern that even the same general principles or ideas are similarly expressed according to qualitative different interpretations.

That is to say, the intrinsic distinction of an entity is not merely a strange intangible coordinate that is not evident in the appearance. But essential significance is physically implied and pertains to the inherent nature of the existence of something. In other words, the characteristic nature of a phenomenon is intangible although represented materially as the manner whereby something is particularly expressed. This is reflected in the representative, qualitative manner whereby a Natural circumstance declares a certain disposition.

The particular, qualitative singularity of the existence of something epitomizes the intrinsic identity because the manner whereby something is expressed reveals the particular nature. Thus, while physical properties pertain to the material status, the intrinsic uniqueness of the existence of a phenomenon concerns the innate distinction. In other words, in the same way as it is with human beings, the outward aspect belies an essential significance.

Furthermore, the material condition of a thing is always temporal. But the crucial significance that is the manner of the expression resides as the integral, discreet distinction that is only distantly represented in the appearance. More precisely, the innate consequence of something is imperceptible from a consideration of the solely material aspect because the appearance does not directly reveal the characteristic demeanor of the manifestation.

However, this does not negate or marginalize the appearance. It merely contrasts semblance with intrinsic distinction or superficial obviousness against implicit significance. Both perspectives are valid although, increasingly, only the physical is ceded existential relevance. Consequently, if we consider the transient, material aspect as the full extent of the existence of something, then our perspective only concerns the issue but not the foundation.

Thus, we cannot know the identity of a phenomenon merely by its temporal appearance because we cannot obviously tell how it qualitatively expresses, yet, it is through the mainstay of the physical that we discern the inherent significance. In other terms, the material is the manifest evidence that establishes a tangible connection and focus for immediate cognition, that would otherwise remain without practical direction.

The Eastern mystic considers the material condition to be illusory. But in reality, the superficial view is the fault of our imperfect manner of cognition whereby we solely recognize the appearance of a phenomenon and overlook the intangible significance. The physical appearance is not illusory, but it is an insufficient representation that incompletely depicts the phenomenon, and the facade is imagined to constitute the entirety.

We do not deny the existence of the appearance. To do so typifies the remoteness of the practice of abstract reasoning whereby one pursues a logical sequence of deduction, distant from the event, and attains a conclusion that bears little resemblance to reality. Abstraction does not lead us to a straightforward experience of the reality of phenomena. Only the immediate engagement by the human singularity of existence can achieve direct cognition.

Eastern mysticism remains preoccupied with an

introvert experience of human, individual existence which, through the immediacy of the encounter, is justifiably considered supremely real. This is the opposite approach from materialistic, Western philosophy that cedes exclusive value to the physical appearance and denies the existence of intangible significance. Nevertheless, the material condition is the outer appearance of a more profound existential significance and while even the mystic inevitably concedes that the physical exists, although without transcendental merit, we recognize both the essential and dependent conditions.

Furthermore, from the perspective of the principle as opposed to the subsidiary material focus of attention, we discover that the human essential distinction is able to discern the full dimensionality of phenomenal existence. Consequently, the implication of an emphatic point of view is vastly more significant that that of the peripheral outlook.

More simply put, we recognize that the essential meaning of something is overlooked if we consider that the entirety solely occupies the physical appearance and that the material is the extent of any significance. Consequently, through the dismissal of intangible evidence concerning the qualitative, essential constitution of phenomena, we find ourselves circumscribed by a world-view inevitably bereft of importance. In other words, we find that there no purpose in an existence that is merely superficial.

Nevertheless, at fault is our own narrow view and not whether one thing is real and another illusory. Preoccupied with the transient as if alone the passing, impermanent aspect of circumstances comprised reality, it is inevitable that the climate of the human mind is similarly disheartened through a shallow understanding of existence. Consequently, we find that humankind pursues meaning in fugitive circumstances where no substance is to be found.

It is necessary to cease the prevalent indirect, intellectual interpretation of life and engage phenomena immediately in order to attain a fuller and more meaningful understanding. Otherwise, human prospects remain exceedingly bleak. Nevertheless, the dreamy alternative founded upon feeling-sentience and esoteric vagary offers merely a subjective alternative that is similarly abstract, although prone to even greater fantasy.

However, through immediate cognition it is straightforwardly feasible to engage phenomena and recognize the intrinsic significance and actual identity. In other words, if we discern the essential relevance of all things, obviously the human experience becomes proportionately meaningful.

Therefore, when the individual ipseity directly engages something, the immediate approach reveals the intrinsic significance of the phenomena. Thus, for example, organic forms are recognized not merely in terms of their appearances and obvious, physical properties but essentially, for the concepts upon which they are organized and established, and the manner whereby they qualitatively express their existence.

Simply put, immediate engagement through the human essence involves the discovery of the identity of something as it exists substantively. We do not merely examine the superficial appearance nor analyze the material obviousness; we confront the object as it exists independently of human interpretation and designation. Thereby, we discover what a thing is in terms of its intrinsic nature.

Indeed, the intrinsic significance of everything arranged and organized, including a humanly, manufactured object, lies in its conceptual inception. Thus, the relevance of a plant or of a creature is greater than the appearance or the intricate mechanics of growth because the essential pertinence exists as the general archetypal concept, whose specific manner of application is dependent upon the responsive nature and ecological context of the creature.

Similarly, the essential identity of the human being is that which would remain if a person no longer inhabited a body. Stated differently, the intrinsic relevance and singular, individual existence of a person is the selfhood that we meaningfully encounter, and not merely the biological appearance. The materialization offers a point of focus, but significant engagement occurs essentially.

Furthermore, it is the permanence of the human being as an entity that discovers the enduring significance of the phenomenon, through immediate encounter.

For example, the immediate engagement of a man-made object from the perspective of the human ipseity reveals a compound of concepts, the will to realize them physically, and finally, their material manifestation in the form of the finished product. It could even be argued that conceptualization and will were of greater significance than the final product because the article could not exist without precedent, while a concept can exist without being physically realized. Yet, neither conceptualization nor volition exist tangibly but only in the form of their consequence.

Straightforward reasoning of this nature is readily grasped by the intellect. However, it also implicitly describes the actual circumstances of the physical condition and not merely an abstract proposition. More to the point, in reality, the intrinsic condition is the original and enduring significance of a phenomenon.

Conceptualization is known to exist intangibly in terms of a humanly fabricated object. But strangely, when an organism is considered and evaluated, conceptual origin is denied because the existence of conceptualization is physically elusive and there is no practical evidence that it exists. Indeed, materialistic Western philosophy only includes materially verifiable evidence and consequently, the inception of a creature is attributed to the spontaneous repercussions of a limitless passage of time. Nevertheless, even a human idea originates as an intangible phenomenon.

We know full well that the manufactured article began as an idea followed by the intention to realize it physically, and the actual process of making. But we only recognize forethought because we ourselves follow the same procedure and we are very familiar with the sequence of events. However, if we did not know that an article was humanly conceived, through direct cognition we would, nevertheless, discover the original conceptualization and intention.

Human organization requires conceptualization along with the intention to achieve a practical realization. Furthermore, the human, singular selfhood is able to corroborate the existence of a similar precedent prevalent in Nature even though the conceptual architecture is not necessarily apparent. But, in a similar way, while the human designer may be absent, nevertheless, we accept that someone was behind the arrangement, for example of Stonehenge, in Wiltshire, England. We accept that long-ago architects exercised their will towards its realization.

The source of Natural organization is similarly unknown but, strangely, we do not willingly credit the organic situation with intentional genius. This is because human invention does not require the presence of a designer since we are familiar with how human structures originate. But we suppose Natural things are either somehow miraculous or that they came into existence through a myriad of unlikely coincidental events.

Indeed, the prevailing evolutionary theory promotes a synchronous, spontaneous beginning upon the unsupported caveat that even the impossible is possible over a limitless time span. Indeed, upon the strength of this abstract overreach an entire biographical progression has been both contrived and accepted by erudite academia. In view of this, one wonders how far the scholarly approach really differs from a belief in the magical.

However, if someone, ignorant of the existence of a concept, were able to conclusively reason that a humanly manufactured item possessed both inception and the will to bring it into physical existence, the same deductive operation would similarly find conceptualization and will to be in evidence in Nature. Consequently, at the foundation of the contention between evolution and creationism, we discover not empirically derived evidence, but very human partiality.

In other words, the intangible origin of a humanly fabricated object is accepted. But it is disavowed in terms of living Nature because of an established prejudice that prevents the universal application of the same, simple logic. This not only reveals the selective nature of human rationale, but demonstrates how removed philosophy is from the precision of calculation.

In the same vein, an argument cannot be reduced into piecemeal fractions in order to be more easily predictable because in terms of rationale, the precise calculation of mathematics is incommensurate. That is to say, proposals concerning the entirety do not remain the same upon reduction, they are merely reduced into different whole arguments. Similarly, the circumstances of the detail of something cannot be extrapolated into comprehensive, existential philosophy because the part does not explain the entirety but only the circumstances of the particular aspect.

In terms of the superficial appearance as opposed to the substantive significance of things, nobody would seriously deny that a man-made object consists of more than the physical properties and functions because we ourselves commence invention through the establishment a compound of related concepts and we exercise our will and practical expertise to realize them. Thus, from our own experience we know that this is the manner whereby something is made even though the creative forces exist intangibly within our mind. However, if we attempt to reason whether a man-made object is produced in this way, it would also be possible to argue that such was not the case. We might even present convincing evidence that the object spontaneously arose through the influence of natural forces, over vast eons. Indeed, we could suggest any abstract proposition that we desire to imagine, such is the fallibility of rationale.

The manner whereby we can discern the distinction between fantasy and reality has more to do with perspective than with commonsense. Unfortunately, we can be persuaded by argumentation that the imaginary really exists unless we have an established benchmark that demonstrates unequivocal certainty. Indeed, as we have already discussed, mathematics is ideal but inapplicable in existential and philosophical terms. Furthermore, rationale and religious conviction both fail to offer definitive knowledge, the latter because it is a belief and the former because reason operates indirectly.

The intellect is a function without identity and, consequently, it cannot experience. It is only through direct engagement by the human singularity of existence, that definitive knowledge concerning the existential significance of something, is decisively achieved. In other words, existential identification is beyond the capacity of the reasoning faculty because the intellect cannot directly encounter a phenomenon and discover its significance. It can only decisively deduce in relation to physically verifiable information, derived from the circumstances of the material appearance.

Nevertheless, an organic form, immediately engaged by the human singularity of existence, is experientially recognized in terms of its conceptual origin and the volition behind its physical realization.

Accordingly, it is through immediacy, that the human essence encounters the phenomenon in the condition of its intrinsic significance because that is what direct engagement implies. Therefore, by immediate engagement, the human essence discovers not more information concerning the superficial properties of a phenomenon but the significance of its existence. That is to say, the intrinsic significance of something is not the physical realization but the profound conceptual nature and the respective expression of its existence.

Furthermore, the consequences of immediate cognition are definitive because thereby we discern the essential circumstances, and the perspective of our observation is in like manner, essential and unimpaired.

The intrinsic circumstances of human existence are essentially consistent irrespective of the shallowness of our point of view. But if our perspective is cursory, inevitably, our entire experience will be correspondingly insufficient. However, in order to intensify our perception and comprehension, the determination to observe more fully will only serve laterally but not necessarily in terms of profundity. In other words, in order to establish a more profound view, we require an approach that offers not greater knowledge, but a more perceptive engagement.

For example, a color may be interpreted emotionally, but the communication would be markedly different depending on the view of the individual observer. However, intrinsically a color will always possess the identical significance regardless how it may be subjectively depicted. But both subjective interpretation and physical analysis as far as it goes, does not reveal the intrinsic identity. There is only one identity for a particular color, and it is discovered as the qualitative distinction or manner of its existence..

Thus, we recognize how remote and removed observation and evaluation usually are from the actual condition of existence and how extraordinarily abstract and oblique the perfunctory interpretation of color is, whether it is numerically described or somehow depicted in terms of a wavelength.

Indeed, a systematic methodology does not offer definitive knowledge irrespectively of the application but only evaluates the significance of specifically amenable data. Consequently, a physical scientific approach is incommensurate with philosophy, but appropriate to material investigation. But if we apply the limited conclusions of the physicist to existence, we thereby project a specialized perspective as an overview, where it has no jurisdiction.

In this connection, the materialistic, Western philosophical understanding of existence is almost entirely preoccupied with the physical. Even the painstaking scrutiny of phenomena remains shallowly confined to only consequential evidence because of an exclusive attention towards the material repercussions. Therefore, the intangible, qualitative dimension is given scant regard because its existence is unverifiable in corporeal terms. Nevertheless, at the very least, qualities are known to be real even though they are intangible. However, their existence does not alter an exclusively, physical philosophy one iota. Thus, the profound significance of intangible qualification remains unacknowledged.

Therefore, it is incumbent upon the individual to discover the implication of the qualitative proportion of physical conditions. At first, we may agree with the shallow perspective and suppose that physically elusive modification is, indeed, existentially negligible. But physical science cannot help us in our understanding because material exclusiveness is correspondingly constricted within tangible parameters even though scientism has successfully encroached upon philosophy and effectively marginalized metaphysics.

Nevertheless, the qualitative significance of a physical phenomenon is the manner according to which a thing is intrinsically identifiable. Consequently, we recognize the shallowness of the exclusively material approach. Materialism solely considers the ramifications of the obvious appearance; not the intrinsic nature whereby something is expressed.

Through a consideration of the foregoing paragraph, we can recognize by comparison what happens to our understanding of a phenomenon if the intrinsic nature is dismissed. Suddenly, we see only an empty husk because both particular relevance and essential meaning are gone if something is denied qualitative differentiation. In essence the pertinence of the object ceases to exist in our understanding because the qualitative significance of a phenomenon, that is the intrinsic nature, is the more profound proportion.

However, if we engage the intrinsic significance of something separately from the physical circumstances, we find existence populated with individualized, existential expression.

In the same vein, we seldom negotiate many things that we deal with in everyday life beyond the associations that accompany the names that have been previously allocated. Consequently, we may never discover the intrinsic nomen that describes the characteristic expression of something, and our perception remains heedless.

Thus, the immediate experience and acknowledgement of one's own, essential existence are commonly thought too discretionary because physically elusive conditions, frequently, in our time, are considered unlikely. Nevertheless, the human essence is intangible and alike to all qualitative existence it must be experientially encountered in order to be known. Consequently, it comes of no surprise to find the human ipseity excluded from the abstract, materialistic perspective wherein everything is adjudged by its physical presence and only the material properties are considered significant.

Therefore, it follows that if qualitative, experientially apprehended information is considered of marginal significance and denied relevance within a world-view that is founded upon solely physically established facts, then it is very unlikely that the human, essential existence will find relevance within such a philosophy.

But it is, ironically, through a logical examination of qualitative significance that the flaw of an exclusively, materially founded philosophy is discovered. Once it is accepted that a neglected, intangible dimension to life, nevertheless, exists in spite of the insistence of the determined materialist, then further experiential research becomes possible. Subsequently, if the qualitative dimension of existence is accepted as authentic through experiential cognition, it becomes an easy step to similarly apply the straightforward approach and discover one's own essential existence. Once we have obtained direct knowledge of our individual incorporeal significance, the authentic condition of things becomes apparent from the same perspective.

It is obvious that this simple, successive examination that the significance of intangible reality is only feasible if the researcher sets aside pre-conceptual and prejudicial bias and engages phenomena uniquely. But if it is imagined that we already possess an answer to an existential question that is, in fact, beyond our cognitive ability to attain, then a more profound perspective, such as immediate cognition remains an unconvincing and unnecessary alternative.

Nevertheless, the distinction between conventional cognition, whereby a situation is abstractly evaluated, and the approach of immediate engagement lies in the profundity. That is to say, immediacy presents a different perspective from intellectual or emotional evaluation because it involves explicitness.

For example, if we consider Native Element Minerals superficially for their physical properties, and endeavor to understand and classify them systematically, we only attain evidence of their material condition. However, when copper or silver is directly and experientially encountered, we discover the intrinsic significance that substantively distinguishes one Element from another.

We find that the essential distinctions between them are qualitative and intangible. Accordingly, silver is found to consist of an inherent, characteristic significance that is incomprehensible in physical terms. On the other hand, copper is discovered to be of an entirely different nature, the quality of which is immediately evident when we engage the two in comparison and restrain from describing them in terms of the properties and appearance. In other words, every Native Element Mineral possesses an intrinsic, intangible significance that only becomes evident when the human essence immediately and experientially engages the physical appearance.

Therefore, the crux of immediate cognition whereby the essential existence of something may be recognized, is composed of several features: In order to proceed effectively, we must recognize that the qualitative dimension of existence is profound. We do this by postponing the conventional abstract interpretation of life that has subsumed the actual thing, and thereby we recognize that experientially determined qualities possess a unique existence.

Therefore, in order to discover the qualitative uniqueness of a phenomenon, we must engage it experientially because our reasoning faculties and our emotional preferences will otherwise obscure its significance. Consequently, through the experientially justified recognition of the authenticity of the intangible, qualitative dimension of existence, we turn our attention to our own essence.

Once our essential identity is experientially discovered to be authentic through the immediacy of the approach, we establish the human essence as the perspective from which to regard other people and phenomenal existence.

In short, the condition of immediacy is a significant approach in terms of the opposition to abstract or emotional cognition, which always evaluates indirectly. Thus, while materialistic, Western philosophy has marginalized qualities as more or less existentially insignificant and imagines that we are exclusively reasoning and emotional creatures, we discover for ourselves a deeper profundity.

The contrast between rationalization in order to achieve existential knowledge and the cognitive condition of immediacy, reveals the difference between the abstract construction and the profound. That is, immediacy involves direct cognition between the human essential existence and a phenomenon, in present time, without the distortions of theoretical constructs that masquerade as definitive knowledge.

Unfortunately, we exist in a counterfeit chimerical condition of our own making. We imagine things to be other than they are in reality. This misconception is clearly recognized when abstract thinking is superseded by immediate engagement. Thereby, phenomena are discovered for their intrinsic significance, while what we think of them or imagine them to be, is found to be irrelevant. Thus, abstract evaluation is restored within appropriate parameters and it no longer attempts to imagine what reality is but it occupies itself inventively. Thus, increasingly, we become cognitively autonomous to the degree that we recognize the way things exist in reality.

9. The Neglected Dimension

René Descartes considered the inconsistent nature of the information attainable through the human, physical senses as indicative of our incapacity to unequivocally confirm the very existence of a physical realm. He arrived at this position of skepticism through abstract conjecture. Logically, it seems conceivable that if the constitution of sensory information is found to be inconsistent, then, it throws the value of all sense-derived knowledge into doubt.

However, it is of marginal importance whether the human senses convey accurate information concerning a phenomenon or if, as René Descartes suggested, they reveal only subjective intelligence and general indicators. Indeed, it is self-evident that the senses cannot reveal definitive or absolutely accurate knowledge concerning an object of scrutiny not only because the senses are individually specific, but also the material portion of things is the least substantive.

Accordingly, the one individual will see a certain color somewhat differently from another because the quality of vision remains dependent upon individual body variances, and the subjective interpretation of each individual is similarly characteristic. In a similar vein, the superficial proportion of a phenomenon does not require exactitude in order to be cursorily identified. Indeed, if we wish to explore the physical appearance with exactitude then we must independently measure and calibrate the material properties of phenomena. Yet, otherwise, the essential significance and intrinsic identity of something is discerned through an entirely different metric.

The value of Descartes rationale is more that it demonstrates the fallibility of abstract conjecture and shows how the imagination can function remotely, and in isolation from experientially engaged and empirically verified existence. The abstraction of Descartes reveals the disconnectedness of speculative philosophy, from reality.

Abstraction is the extrapolation of a reasonable assumption beyond recognized, governing coordinates. But the difficulty lies in the establishment of an absolute benchmark according to which all things might be compared and correlated. In mathematics, this is straightforward because the accountant can always return to a prior summation. But in terms of philosophy, the representative standard must be existentially indisputable. That is to say, the premise of a philosophy or a religion must be established upon absolutes.

However, in terms of the findings of immediate cognition, direct engagement presupposes the absence of abstract conjecture, and consequently the ipseity itself supplies the requisite existential certainty.

Indeed, it is irrelevant to the discovery of the intrinsic identity of something, or to the recognition of the essential existence of another person, whether the senses offer the exact same evidence or if the cumulative sensory impression of something varies between individuals. That is to say, it is not the material condition alone that interests us, but the existential significance of the phenomenon: the appearance coordinates our attention but it is the intrinsic nature that we would discover.

In other terms, immediate engagement does not strive to discover the exact nature of the physical appearance, but the innate distinction of something. The appearance merely anchors the attention upon a particular event. Yet, for its part, the human ipseity exists inextricably with the essential of things, and consequently it is concerned with the similarly essential dimension of the existence of a phenomenon, that otherwise remains physically unrepresented.

René Descartes was concerned that the existence of the material world was unverifiable because the senses could not provide conclusive intelligence. Ironically, the physical appearances of phenomena solely represent their outward and most blatant condition, while the intrinsic existence remains indiscoverable through sensory perception alone. That is to say, knowledge concerning the superficial is always influenced by the perspective of the observer. But intrinsic significance exists of itself, independently of the point of view.

In order to determine the intrinsic identity of something, the essential, human singularity must assert its cognitional authority over intellectual evaluation and emotion bias, and overlook the apparent evidence presented by the physical senses. This does not imply that the material appearance does not exist but that it merely represents the most obvious and superficial aspect. However, the direct experience of the intrinsic existence of something is achieved, not intellectually through abstract rationale, but by means of immediate engagement. That is, the essential existence of something is discovered through a direct encounter with the appearance. Yet, the substantive distinction exists incorporeally, as the intrinsic entirety of the phenomenon. Hence, if the testimony of the senses varies, it is of little importance in terms of the inherent existence of something.

As adults, we are highly familiar with material conditions although very young children have much to learn in order to navigate between them. However, reference to human and essential incorporeality no doubt strikes the reader as an unreasonable postulate. Nevertheless, the most meaningful aspects of life are most frequently those without physical representation, and consequently they must be poetically described in order to be adequately portrayed.

Thus, human intelligence is not a victim of the apparently undependable nature of the senses, but it is the master over sensory findings. The senses provide a wide variety of perspectives concerning an object, but it is the Mind that sorts and evaluates the information and makes meaning of it. Nevertheless, if we wish to attain a more profound view and discern the essential significance of things, the usual evaluative approaches must be restrained in order that the ipseity may establish an unimpeded prospect.

However, the intellect manages information only after the sensory event, and calculates hypothetically and imaginatively, while striving to achieve decisive knowledge. Yet, the distinction between the abstract evaluation of something and definitive knowledge concerning its essential existence, lies in the profundity of the engagement. A phenomenon that is only superficially regarded and casually assessed upon the merits of its appearance, is merely peripherally identified and its intrinsic significance remains obscure.

Similarly, if the appearance of an object is examined with careful scrutiny, systematically analyzed, labeled and its workings meticulously observed, it is the details of the physical condition alone that are discovered, but not the inherent identity.

In order that the essential existence of a phenomenon may be apprehended, the human essence must directly engage the physical appearance, through the aegis of its own significance. In other words, lateral astute rationale and oblique evaluation, including feeling-sentience, will not suffice. Thereby, we merely apply more intensity to the same approach. But the condition of immediacy wherein the object and the human essence coincide, is discovered when the subjective and superficial evaluation of something is postponed, in order that the human essence may directly engage without obstruction or interference from indirect evaluation.

Engagement through the human essence is not subjective but involves a quality of cognition wherein the object is directly engaged and identified for its intrinsic existence. It is apprehended without intermediary conceptualization. It is neither interpreted nor evaluated, but straightforwardly encountered and consequently discovered and identified as it exists intrinsically.

In contrast, the superficial approach is of little value in terms of intrinsic identification because it provides merely cursory evidence and does not involve the intrinsic relevance. A partial and biased perspective may be our conventional approach but, nonetheless, it remains inadequate because it fails to indicate what something is essentially, and it avoids the greater, intangible significance of the phenomenon.

To stress once more, a thorough scrutiny and analysis of the physical appearance inevitably disappoints because the intrinsic consequence of something does not reside in the material expression but it is only implied through the image. The physical is not the entirety of the phenomenon. Indeed, the isolated appearance is entirely without intrinsic significance on its own because the intangible value of its qualitative distinction, unique identity and conceptual origin, are the essential meaning and the significant dimension of a thing.

The capacity to discover the profound, incorporeal existence of a phenomenon is exclusively possessed by the human essence. That is, the substantive significance of all things reside in the same intangible condition. Consequently, the essential human being is able to directly discern the innate distinction of all other phenomena.

However, the representation of intrinsic existence is physically indeterminable because while implied in the form, it exists intrinsically. Consequently, we recognize that the inherent identity of a phenomenon is imperceptible through either subjective cognition or the detailed analysis of the physical properties. This is attributable, not to the inadequacy of sensory information but because appearances, cognitively isolated from their inherent distinction, do not in themselves possess essential significance. Therefore, the intrinsic identity of something cannot be found merely in the physical structure, but it is discovered within the otherwise neglected dimension of immediacy.

In other words, intrinsic identity is distinguished from the physical appearance of a phenomenon, through its existential expression. Consequently, a property or physical aspect does not possess the identity of the entirety but it merely compounds the material aggregate. Nevertheless, distinctive particularity exists immanently as the entirety of the existential expression of a phenomenon. Similarly, the physical properties of something are dependent upon the intrinsic identity but they are not equivalent to it. This is because, the essential significance of something is physically elusive, and it is only found through immediate engagement by the human essence.

That is to say, the inherent distinction of something is conspicuous from the physical appearance through the intangible nature of its existence. Thus, when an object is described in terms of the physically elusive qualities one approaches the inherent distinction. But in order to avoid a merely subjective appraisal it is vital to engage the object directly from the perspective of unalloyed inquiry. However, the human ipseity is the essential identity of the human constitution and through immediacy, it experiences things definitively and not interpretatively.

10. At Odds with Experience

Materialistic, Western philosophy has increasingly become a firmly established perspective towards life even though it remains a construct at odds with experience. This should not matter because, of course, everyone is entitled to an opinion. However, the difficulty concerns not only the pervasive propagation of a paricular ideology but the manner whereby the materialistic perspective precedes research. That is to say, in much the same way as any religion, when doctrine anticipates the conclusion it thereby blocks openminded access.

For example, exclusive materialism requires that human identity should correspond with physical circumstances. Yet individual, essential significance is not corporeal but exists immediately and immanently. Consequently, the skeptic attributes individuality to a biological organ and supposes that brain activity premises the suggestion of a physically elusive origin. Furthermore, the body is thought to comprise the full extent of the person even though the structure is mortal. Consequently, the human being is assumed to be similarly temporal; a presupposition with harmful psychological implications.

The reason for the appeal of physicalism lies in the apparently substantial foundation that the material appearance of things provides. But it is incorrectly surmised that the appearance is the entirety of the phenomenon. As we have already explored, the existence of an albeit marginalized, qualitative significance that epitomizes the distinction of phenomena undermines the exclusive reliance upon physically derived evidence. Consequently, materialism is revealed as an insufficient philosophy because of the selective nature of the intelligence upon which it is established. Thus, if the intrinsic expression that essentially identifies things is excluded and only the physical appearance is considered, then materialism is immediately recognized as prejudiced and contrived because it fails to correspond with actual circumstances.

Simply put, the qualitative distinction and intrinsic expression of the existence of a phenomenon precede the physical in significance. For example, corporeal magnitude and physical proportion are incommensurate assessments in terms of the essential nature. Consequently, it is possible for a tiny shrew to possess the courage of a lion and a much larger animal to fearfully shun daylight and exposure.

Accordingly, while the qualitative dimension of a phenomenon is obviously physically indefinable its value is far from negligible as we know from our own practical experience. However, the stalwart champion of materialism will claim that the qualitative nature of something is of minimal importance because it can only be subjectively determined. Indeed, it is certainly recognized that qualities, values and intangible significances exist but because they are only capriciously identified and evaluated, they do not seem to significantly compare with tangible conditions.

This is a convenient evasion and typical of the abstract mentality that does not engage phenomena empirically but tries to hypothetically reason the nature of existence. In reality, when intangible values are experientially confronted, it is immediately evident that they are of enormous practical significance.

However, the quality of something bears little resemblance to the physical appearance of a phenomenon, which is of an entirely different nature. Yet, the physical appearance is impossible to avoid, but the qualitative significance of an object is experientially inescapable even though it remains physically elusive. Furthermore, although, through abstract polemic, intangible value is excluded from a materialistic philosophical appraisal of life, in practice its importance is self-evident. Everything possesses caliber, character and value distinction without which it would be as if language were without adjectives, adverbs and metaphors.

Indeed, in any moment, we can experientially justify for ourselves that the qualitative dimension of phenomena is as significant as the physical appearance. Consequently, if we imagine life without quality and value we are confronted with a conjectural impression that fails to correspond with the world that we know. Further, upon careful examination it will be found that the qualitative counterpart of the physical semblance is of greater consequence than the appearance because the authentic identity of the phenomenon resides within the intangible merit.

Upon the inclusion of the qualitative volume of existence, the influence of materialistic, Western philosophy is profoundly contradicted by successfully reducing the exclusive emphasis upon material relevance, and expanding the importance of the incorporeal significance. Suddenly, existence is not merely composed of physical properties, but it is vastly enlarged through the inclusion of the qualitative proportion.

Unfortunately, qualities possess no independent physicality nor can they be successfully rendered numerically and quantified. Logically, it is extremely difficult to construct an abstract world-view wherein everything possesses qualitative value, because qualities must be experienced directly in order to be recognized. Nevertheless, intellectual constructions inevitably avoid experiential evidence concerning the intangible nature of things because they simply cannot be successfully assimilated within a serious abstract philosophy. Abstract rationale is consequently an inadequate approach towards a comprehensive view of life because a significant aspect of existence, while experientially recognized, cannot be intellectually adjudicated as extant.

Therefore, intangible significances are intellectually dismissed as subjective whimsy or merely deemed an enhancement to the physical appearance and considered to be without further importance. They are not credited with meaningful value and are consequently excluded as evidence towards an understanding of existence. Thus, the material condition of things is established as supreme, and even though we constantly experience qualities, they do not alter the materialistically founded exclusivity that insists upon a view of existence at odds with our own experience.

The argument that maintains that the qualitative value of a phenomenon can only be subjectively identified and evaluated, has some merit when qualities, values, and the character of things are merely engaged emotionally and evaluated casually. But the same misgiving holds true for materially derived evidence. If the physical appearance of something is adjudged only superficially, then the forthcoming evidence is similarly, of little consequence in terms of a comprehensive philosophy of life. But, unlike the intangible significance of something, physical properties can be further scrutinized and extensively systemized, and categorized according to their minutest detail. The qualitative dimension of phenomena, however, receives scant attention and is relegated to the instinctive and intuitive realm.

Neglect of the qualitative dimension and the overemphasis of the physical is the inevitable consequence of an abstractly contrived position because intangible significances cannot be evaluated in the same manner as the physical. That is to say, physical properties are easy to quantify and measure, and they may be conveniently categorized, but the elusive, qualitative significance of a phenomenon is described only through considerable and demanding illustration. Furthermore, the physical aspects of something are most readily evidenced and accordingly they receive far greater attention than the intangible value.

Indeed, it is very difficult to succinctly communicate the quality or value of something, and intangibles do not lend themselves successfully to assimilation in materialistic terms. The problem is compounded because the medium whereby incorporeal existence is ideally revealed and conveyed is art.

Unfortunately, art has degenerated in our time to a dilettante expression of emotional conditions and of patterns, colors or haunting, but otherwise meaningless verse. It has been thoroughly commercialized so that it less resembles a language whereby the qualitative dimension of existence is revealed, but it is reduced instead to the status of a commodity. Thereby, art has lost the significance and responsibility that it formerly possessed as a vernacular describing physically elusive existence.

This entrenched, present-day, superficial mentality appears to exist without significant challenge or alternative. Therefore, the determination of the abstract materialist faces an easy opposition against experiential but frequently subjective knowledge that does not seriously contradict an established philosophy because essential significances cannot be physically proven to exist.

Consequently, the human perspective becomes increasing weighted towards material evidence, so that even the religious perspective, that purports to explain an incorporeal existence, is frequently revealed as strongly materialistic in essence. Indeed, the orthodox devout are frequently more concerned with corporeal, social and doctrinal matters rather than the qualitative advancement of the soul.

However, when phenomena are immediately experienced it is unnecessary to establish an abstract world-view, nor to construct an explanatory conceptualization of existence. This means that materialistic, Western philosophy is revealed as moot in the light of immediate engagement because we encounter things as they exist intrinsically, in the entirety of their significance, and we recognize their definitive existence through direct experience. That is to say, we do not require an interpretive construct to explain life when we know the reality for ourselves without intermediary explanation.

A world-view that is solely, materially founded endeavors to evaluate phenomena based upon their physical appearance. Consequently, the conclusions of materialistically established reasoning are bound to be exclusively pertinent to the physical aspects and properties of things. This is incredibly depressing, but it is not ultimately damaging that we have erred on the side of a materialistic interpretation of existence if conventional cognition is eventually superseded by immediate engagement through the perspective of the human essence.

In other words, the practice of immediate cognition must rely upon the physical in order to anchor its attention upon a specific phenomenon and avoid drifting into pure fantasy. This is because, typically, the present alternative response to materialism is a position estranged from reality, ill-founded and fanciful and impossible to verify. To abandon the materialistic perspective for the vagueness of wishful thinking, or for constructs founded upon esoteric mythology, is no progress at all. Nevertheless, while materialism at least spares us the indulgence of superstition, magic and supernatural extravagance, it remains similarly misguided unless the intrinsic and more profound value of phenomena are justified as both extant and philosophically important.

Conventionally, an object may be demonstrated as existent through sensory derived information concerning it, and further qualified because the physical properties can be calibrated in a variety of ways. Thereby, the careful scrutiny and measurement of the appearance of an object appear to justify its existence. However, in reality it merely qualifies the physical appearance, the existence of which we do not deny. But a conflict arises when the entirety of the object is claimed to be represented by the material condition. Overlooked is the qualitative particularities that distinguish phenomena, the unique identity that defines them and, indeed, the conceptual origin of organic organization.

Further, the abstract thinker philosophically elaborates the physical properties, extrapolates and generalizes them almost as if they possessed existence independently of the phenomenon itself. Nevertheless, the hypothetical, abstract excursion towards fiction, that entertains a circumstance in which the physical properties of a phenomenon exist independently of the essence, is something that is, in reality, impossible. That is to say, properties have no pertinence without an entirety, and an object is meaningless without intrinsic significance.

Nevertheless, the purely academic conclusions are entertained as reasonable and even probable, which is an alarming indication of how far we have erred through abstract conjecture. Thus, an exclusively material perspective is philosophically extrapolated upon evidence concerning the physical condition of an isolated phenomenon that in reality it does not exist in an autonomous condition in any reasonably definable manner that can be expanded to represent the entirety of existence.

However, the essential distinction of a physical object exists intangibly alike to the qualitative variations that intrinsically distinguish one thing from another. It is the essential distinction that we wish to know because it enlarges an otherwise exclusively physical assessment of existence and completes it with meaning and relevance. In other words, the solely physical, peripheral existence of something is enhanced through intrinsic knowledge, but an understanding of the significance does not detract from the superficial, it enhances it.

The exclusively material perspective offers a view of existence that does not exist in reality, and a philosophy established on a constricted view is merely an abstractly contrived supposition. Material exclusivity contradicts experientially derived intelligence and presents a sterile, counterfeit semblance of existence. Therefore, things are distinguished from one another based upon their appearances and not in terms of their intrinsic distinction.

Thus, for example, physical analysis finds no critical difference between certain foods that are otherwise remote from each other through a qualitative disparity that indicates nutritional as opposed to chemical composition. Essentially, however, the consumer can differentiate very easily between factory-farmed produce and sun-ripened organic fruits and vegetables. But qualitative distinctions are not readily calibrated or identified in physical terms and, consequently, they seem obscure and subjectively derived. Consequently, they are severely reduced in significance when compared to evidence derived from an exclusively physical depiction.

However, immediate engagement by the human, essential distinction removes intelligence concerning intrinsic relevance from the realm of uncertainty because the human essence engages phenomena originally, not merely subjectively. That is, the individual ipseity exists in a condition that is not materially confined, and from the greater perspective the profundity of circumstances is readily discerned. Yet, this is not some mysterious situation but merely reveals the neglected proportion of existence that is obscured through a philosophy of materialistic exclusivity.

In other words, unlike the peripheral view, the intrinsic significance of the existence of things is the most profound condition. Yet, it is not one that is only imaginatively sustained or established upon a fanciful presentiment or subjective assessment. But, we discover the intrinsic significance of things through immediate cognition, and thereby, we recognize that an interpretation of existence upon a narrow view is almost entirely at odds with reality. That is to say, the profound view identifies the existential distinction with certainty because it engages circumstances straightforwardly and thereby recognizes the foundational relevance of things that is the innate nomen.

11. The Original Condition

Everything of existential value that reveals the intrinsic identity of phenomena, exists intangibly but, through an overemphasis upon the physical appearance, its significance is evaded. Unable to effectively challenge the exclusivity of physically derived evidence concerning existence, the knowledge that we obtain experientially regarding a greater and more profound significance than the obvious presentation, remains confused and uncertain.

The importance of the qualitative value of something as existentially significant is overlooked by the materialist because it is assumed that intangible nuances merely sanction the physical condition and possess no extensive or separate merit. However, as soon as we begin to acknowledge the essential distinction that epitomizes the intrinsic difference between things, we come to realize that it is the physically elusive characteristics that reveal the substantive significance of phenomena. We find that the material appearance is of lesser profundity because it manifests only the superficial surface and cannot provide information regarding the innate circumstances.

That is to say, our attention is focused by virtue of the outward semblance but in order to discover the intrinsic significance of something the human ipseity must engage a phenomenon directly. Thus, a thorough appreciation is unattainable merely through the scrutiny of the appearance, and we draw no closer to existential knowledge concerning something solely by analyzing the outer covering. Thereby, we merely understand more concerning the periphery.

Humanity has come to believe that material existence alone is worthy of thorough consideration in order to establish a scrupulous, practical philosophy towards life. Therefore, the researcher relies upon intellectual skill to reason a viable construct that encompasses the physically pertinent intelligence that is accumulated. Vaguely a nuance of qualitative inference is permitted, but one cannot successfully demonstrate the authenticity of intangible phenomena from a purely material point of view, therefore elusive subtleties are more or less dismissed the final assessment.

The fault lies in our hesitancy to recognize the significance of the qualitative dimension and to explore the implications of its existence with as much attention as we have given to the prominent appearance. Consequently, a contradiction confronts us between an exclusively material interpretation of life, that insists upon the authority of physical evidence, and the suspicion that the neglected, qualitative dimension is somehow, profoundly significant. With regret, we feel we have lost something of importance through our exclusive emphasis on the physical appearance of things.

Unfortunately, it appears as if nothing can remedy

this situation. We cannot argue against materialism because our own evidence is only experientially acquired and beyond physical justification. In addition, if we initiate a belief system or assume an existing perspective, we are no better off than before because a belief in intangible significances cannot be materially qualified. Try as we may, it remains a significant struggle to remedy the discrepancy between entrenched, materialistic, Western philosophy and our own immediate experience of qualitative significances.

It helps to recognize that exclusive materialism is a superficial philosophical construct that only addresses the carapace of phenomena. In other words, the conclusions of a painstaking analysis of the outward circumstances of things is justified, but only in terms of the least significant countenance. That is to say, materialistic Western philosophy is concerned with the most obvious evidence concerning phenomena and neglects everything that is physically unrepresented. In that sense materialism is a shallow perspective and when recognized as such, does not need to be refuted.

Specifically, that which returns profundity and dimension to existence is not necessarily the establishment of a contradictory doctrine, but the discovery and exploration of the intrinsic significance of things. Indeed, the distinction between the shallow view and perceptive discernment significantly explains much human confusion and subsequent discouragement.

The ultimate reality of the human constitution is the singular existence of every individual. Our actuality is discovered through immediate experience and the authenticity of unique significance is qualified through direct self-engagement, without the intermediary influence of the intellect or feeling-sentience.

In other words, with the restraint of abstract and subjective interpretation, circumstances can be directly engaged from the essential perspective of the human ipseity. Therefore, a phenomenon, directly encountered by the singular existence of the human being, is discovered to exist differently than otherwise represented on the exclusive basis of the physical appearance. Consequently, it is hardly surprising that a philosophy of material preponderance should precipitate unhappiness when only the facile is considered significant.

Immediacy is a condition of engagement unhampered by any intermediary and consequently it is neither involves an interpretation nor a fabricated representation of existence, but it is the direct engagement of the essential condition itself.

In other words, directness as opposed to intellectual abstraction reveals the intangible condition occupied by the human, singular existence. By virtue of immediate engagement, phenomena are discovered not as the prevalent, materialistic, philosophical construct prejudicially interprets them to be, but as they conclusively exist.

A phenomenon is certainly, correctly situated through its physical condition but the observation of appearances alone is insufficient to determine the inherent identity. That is, by immediate engagement, it is found that there exists a qualitative distinction between phenomena, that is unrepresented by the physical condition. This recognition is possible because the human, singular existence upon immediate encounter, is able to experience in terms of the entire significance of something. Indeed, without immediate engagement through the untarnished perspective the human, singular identity, cognition will always remain an oblique practice unable to decisively identify phenomena and always occupied with the merely superficial conditions.

To identify things for their intrinsic distinction of identity and discover the condition in which they exist in totality, a superior manner of cognition than our conventional approach is necessary. Currently, although a systematic approach to research, founded upon physical evidence, remains our primary source of philosophical understanding, it fails to deliver definitive knowledge because the essential existence of something does not reside solely in the appearance.

Looking at a tree, we discover through the unalloyed, immediate engagement of our intrinsic existence, the essential consequence of the phenomenon; one discerns by means of the immediacy of experiential engagement from the perspective of the ipseity, the

111

profound condition in which the inherent distinction of a thing resides. This is an unusual perspective because formerly, we had seldom approached phenomena on their own terms but we had usually, either evaluated them from the position of what we imagined we already knew, or from the perspective of a prevalent conviction, in an emotionally influenced manner.

Immediate engagement from the perspective of our singular and intrinsic existence allows us to encounter cicumstances in the condition in which they fully exist. However, it should not be imagined that profoundness is discovered through direct experience alone. The substantive view is only attainable through the aegis of the human essence because our own intrinsic existence resides in the same fundamental condition as that of the phenomenon. Thus, when the human, singular existence engages a thing immediately, the phenomenon is experienced in the condition of its existential originality.

Observing a tree through immediate cognition, it is astonishing to recognize the distinction between the former, cursory approach and that of immediacy. For one thing, the fact alone of arboreal existence as a reality stands out as a vivid realization. Furthermore, not only is a universal biography evident, but the manner of the particular interpretation of a more narrowly expressed principle becomes apparent. That is to say, we grasp not conceptually but experientially that all trees share essential, archetypal standards expressed qualitatively in markedly different ways. Indeed, it is not hard to identify how each particular variety possess a qualitative distinction whereby it realizes particularly an otherwise general, tree concept, and upon that basis alone the essential nomen is appropriately determined.

Simply put, the oak is distinguished from the maple by the characteristic manner in which each expresses a mutual, archetypal standard. But, of equal importance to this exploration, we discover through immediate engagement the blatant different between a shallow understanding and full cognition. Indeed, it is as if irrespective of an assumed knowledge of trees; we had never before seen such a thing.

In other words, by comparison, the oblique, intellectual consideration of Nature inevitably simplifies and minimizes because it merely studies the periphery. But through immediate engagement we avoid reducing existence to hypothetical structures and convenient, but contrived, constructs because the human singularity encounters phenomena in the condition in which they substantively exist. Therefore, the crux of direct cognition, through the perspective of the human ipseity, lies in the immediacy of the approach and the discovery of the intangible profundity of the existence of the human individual and of all phenomena.

12. Immediately Ascertained Knowledge

The qualitative significance of phenomena reveals the intrinsic distinction when the human ipseity immediately engages them without intellectual or emotional distortion. Straightforwardly encountering a phenomenon, the human essence discovers the essential particularity. Thus, through immediate experience we recognize the independent relevance of a thing and experience it as it occurs without any interpretative or prejudicial involvement from ourselves. Therefore, what a thing intrinsically is becomes evident because the human essence engages it originally.

The quintessential distinction of something is what it is, in and of itself. Consequently, we easily understand that designating an object by virtue of its workings or upon the strength of its composition, misses the intrinsic significance altogether. Indeed, the names that we append originate more typically from cumulative presupposition than from essential knowledge.

However, inherent within the intrinsic circumstances of phenomena resides the meaning and significance concerning their existence. Furthermore, the quiddity can be ascertained by immediate cognition. This is possible because, through immediate engagement, the human essence discerns the existential circumstances in which things profoundly reside. The ipseity as the most profound level of human identification, is able to accomplish this knowledge because it also exists essentially. Thus, recognizing how things are intrinsically, in their most fundamental condition of existence, we discover phenomena as they exist under their own terms and not as we presume them to be.

Indeed, the immediate experience of phenomena, from the perspective of the human essence, banishes the need for conjecture and supposition. Therefore, there is no necessity for humanly contrived structures to explain the way things are because they are immediately encountered in the condition in which they elementally exist. That is to say, the nature of the intrinsic existence of things justifies their own existence and reveals the respective qualitative distinction through the manner whereby they express essential identity merely by being.

Though immediate engagement everything is found as it exists substantively and consequently we do not require interpretation or explanation because things occur as they essentially and entirely are and not as we suppose them to be. But the change that occurs from superficiality to profundity has nothing to do with phenomenon itself, but pertains to our deeper insight and keener perspective.

However, inevitably, without the direct encounter of the human, essential existence, we have to rely upon our own interpretations because we remain ignorant of the intangible significance of phenomena. Consequently, essential knowledge concerning the intrinsic significance of existence remains elusive.

Accordingly, systems that purport to explain existence, although established indirectly through reason or founded upon conviction or belief, remain of a caliber that inevitably falls short of immediately experienced knowledge. Even the apparent emancipation from ideology through an atheistic conviction that purports to be above doctrine and credence, is recognized upon closer examination, to be itself, merely an inverse persuasion. For example, atheism is a disbelief-system, frequently pursued with the comparable vigor and conviction of any other ideology.

Conventionally, our perceptions are misrepresented through shallowness and the oblique manner whereby we endeavor to identify and explain things. Accordingly, the human ipseity seldom engages a phenomenon directly, both because materialistic, Western philosophy regards the individual as corporeally founded, and because the human identity is credited with nothing except general individuality, conditional upon the body. Furthermore, the material condition is purported to comprise the entirety of a thing, and consequently, there is no necessity to explore immediate cognition because it is assumed that there is nothing to discover. Thus, we remain ignorant of the existence of the sovereign, human significance that transcends the physical, and insensitive to the essential manner of its existence. Therefore, the idea of a direct, cognitive approach is virtually meaningless to the materialist and where it is condoned, it is assumed to connote a kind of heightened observation.

However, the direct approach is of far greater significance when the nature of our individual human existence is experientially explored. Thereby, it is found through immediate self-knowledge that the essential identity exists in a permanent condition in which, through immediacy, the authenticity of everything is similarly, directly encountered.

But the effort involved is directed towards restraining intellectual and feeling-sentient interference in order that the consequences of our research remain uninfluenced by abstract speculation and our attention remains immediately focused. However, in terms of knowledge, attentiveness and receptivity is all that is required in order to discern the intrinsic nature of things. In other words, if we wish to discover something entirely unprecedented we must relinquish the presumption of prior understanding and engage circumstances with a completely open mind.

In any event, immediate cognition is not concerned with how something appears physically, or how it may be adjudged and evaluated intellectually or emotionally. But the material circumstances serve to concentrate our attention on the periphery in order to discover the essential of a phenomenon.

All along, the human being has possessed the

capacity to engage intrinsic significances as an inherent capability of our essential existence. Indeed, there would be nothing mysterious about immediate cognition if we had not established a contrary materialistic perspective towards life that interprets everything in terms of the physical appearance. In fact, there is no doubt that abstract conjecture is intellectually convincing, but it is only dislodged through a personal, immediate experience of essentially pertinent circumstances.

Immediate cognition establishes the perspective of the human ipseity through the inhibition of the usual, indirect perceptual practices. From the perspective of our intrinsic identity, we discover the profound nature of the existence of things. However, if it is imagined for a moment that the practice of immediate engagement is a selective or exclusive capability and the province of only a privileged few, we are severely mistaken. That is to say, everyone possesses essential existence; required is the institution of a unique perspective that positions the essential selfhood foremost by the restraint of secondary interpretation.

Philosophically, on the surface, given the physical evidence, we must conclude that humanity is limited to an obvious corporeal condition. However, the implications of this superficial view present only a cheerless prospect, and individually the expectation of a brief and transient lifetime induces a sense of pointlessness. It is upon the strength of the seeming absurdity of these circumstances that we become suspicious that perhaps human existence is being misrepresented.

Indeed, through immediate cognition, we discover that the shallow view inevitably presents a meaningless impression. But upon the discovery of a full volume of formerly overlooked significance, we recognize that the deception rests upon the superficiality of our perspective, and not the way things really are in reality.

In this sense, it seems evident that humanity is slowly awakening from a juvenile mindset circumscribed within very narrow parameters. Indeed, with an increasing recognition of individual ipseity, it becomes blatantly obvious that the condition of singular identity is uniquely and inherently common to everyone. Further, when the unique existence of the human being becomes established as the significant perspective, the existential significance of everything else becomes increasingly evident.

The analogy of the iceberg is perhaps of value here. The significant mass of the mountain resides below the waves while the tip represents only the most obvious proportion. In terms of material conditions, in order to discover the essential, we cannot deny the obvious, but nevertheless, the summit is not the full quantum. Indeed, the pinnacle could not existence without the substantive volume below.

In a similar way, we are determined to discover the

substantive volume in which things essentially reside, and we find that this is possible when our own intrinsic identity is positioned in order to immediately engage something. In particular, we wish to discover what is really going on, and we are ill-content with abstractly contrived explanations, revelations and belief systems that purport to own a monopoly interpretation derived from a narrow, prejudiced point of view.

Those convinced of a particular belief or who are adamant concerning the validity of the abstractly reasoned perspective, insist that they already know the measure of things. But reality is not an explanation of existence or a conceptualized abstraction, but it concerns the authentic existential circumstances discovered through direct experience.

That is to say, profoundness is the imminently accessible state in which things exist irrespectively of what we may otherwise imagine or suppose them to be. Thus, reality is not determined through reason, or revealed through belief or imagination. It is engaged experientially and immediately through our own authentic existence and singular identity, or otherwise, it is not discovered at all.

There exists extensive, intellectual abstraction, pursued systematically through apparently sound reasoning, which is convincingly presented, and we imagine it to be existentially authentic. Through the systematic and logical manner of philosophy whereby

121

various arguments are postulated, a concept may be adopted by consensus as valid, yet remain remote from reality. This is because reason can operate independently and in isolation from authentic existence, remotely managing ideas and abstract constructs. Consequently, reason is purported to be our highest cognitive faculty, yet it functions only indirectly. Thus, we are capable of imagining a condition and skillfully demonstrating its merits even though it may not exist at all. It is even possible, and not infrequent, that extraordinary fabrications are accepted as reasonable for a time, until the contradiction between abstraction and experience reveals a discrepancy with a more favorable understanding.

Similarly, a position need not be entirely abstract, yet it may remain irrelevant because it strives to express a complete perspective while founded merely upon partial evidence. For example, a definition of existence that is exclusively established upon materially derived evidence cannot possibly explain qualitative phenomena. Consequently, as we have already explored, the materialistic depiction of existence remains at odds with common experience because, of necessity, it marginalizes intangible evidence. Thus, a representation of life, devoid of the qualitative dimension of existence cannot possibly resemble our full experience of qualities, values and characteristic, intrinsic distinction, and such a philosophy should make us suspicious.

Fine art serves as a manner of communication whereby something, that is otherwise intangible, may be appropriately described. Otherwise, intangible conditions cannot be successfully revealed in the same manner whereby the blatantly physical properties are accounted. Indeed, the language required to communicate the physical form of an object need only be plain, literal and precise, unadorned by metaphorical characterization. An appearance may be meticulously described without recourse to figurative and descriptive prose. But an artistic medium is required in order to communicate the intrinsic and the profound. However, the significance of art is excluded from materialistic Western philosophy because that which art would communicate is denied real existence. In other words, materialism is both a narrow and superficial perspective.

Unfortunately, a layer of authority is further established through the use of archaic linguistics whereby the minutest physical detail is designated by a Latin or Greek denomination. Consequently, it is difficult to challenge a doctrine if it is concealed through eruditeness and mysterious terminology. Indeed, straightforward observation is discounted by academia and the more enigmatic the exposition the more assured the directorate is of its significance.

For example, materialistic Western philosophy holds that existence consists merely of physically established phenomena. These are easily represented in the dry manner described above. However, if the exclusively physical world-view is authentic, we should not find ourselves as distinctly at odds with it as most people are. Furthermore, something is obviously amiss when the colorful world of our experience is only monochromatically represented.

The moment that an object is described figuratively or in metaphorical terms, something of the intangible dimension of its existence is revealed. It is, of course, entirely possible to represent something fantastic or unsound through figurative speech and intentionally or inadvertently, portray the nonexistent as if it had merit. But the individual, familiar with direct cognition can readily distinguish reality from abstraction, fantasy or a contrived notion. That is to say, experiential engagement through the direct attention of the human essence discovers the manner of the existence of things and becomes steadily more familiar with the tenor of authenticity. Therefore, the contrived position is recognized to be of negligible significance and simply not of the profundity of reality because it does not correspond qualitatively.

Intangible realities, while readily and continuously experienced by everyone, have become relegated as vagaries from the exclusively material point of view. But the high mission of art is to articulate authentic, intangible significances. Thereby, the qualitative dimension of existence, neglected by a simplistic, materialistic interpretation of life, is reintroduced through skillful expression. Consequently, capable artists of every medium can restore our familiarity with intangible existence and elevate the qualitative dimension to renewed significance.

However, there is little intrinsic value to art if the content is illusive to the artist and the articulation of the subject remains obscure to the viewer. The endeavor must be to reveal intangible reality in order that qualitative existence may be demonstrated to be of essential consequence. Of prime significance is the personal experience of essential existence through the perspective of the human essence. Metaphoric and figurative representation necessarily follows experiential knowledge because intangibles otherwise remain obscure and, consequently, incommunicable.

For example, through straightforward encounter, the human ipseity immediately experiences the essential existence of a Native Element Mineral or the intrinsic identity of a color. But as an intangible existence, the essential significance of something cannot be described in material terms because the intrinsic does not possess physical properties. Yet, the inherent significance of gold, copper or silver can be described through metaphoric and figurative representation.

Similarly, the intangible significance and authentic existence of a color can be communicated through movement, music or sculptural form. A finely skilled poet or prose-master can reveal the inherent identity of the same through phrasing and inflection.

That is to say, we engage a phenomenon from the perspective of our own essential perspective and discover the condition of the existence of the object through immediate experience. Indeed, we are already aware of the physical appearance which serves as an anchor and the focus of our attention. But we do not wish to describe the appearance any more than the artist would merely wish to exactly copy a countenance or a landscape. The essential condition is familiar to us, but we cannot articulate it in the same manner whereby its physical appearance is recorded. However, the profound may be eloquently represented through the language of an artistic medium.

The immediate engagement of the essential condition of the existence of a phenomenon is established as a significant experience through the directness of the human self-hood. But feeling assessment and the interpretative evaluation of circumstances that are not physically obvious, is not the same as an immediate engagement by the human ipseity. If the content of a work of art is merely of the former caliber, it will be essentially subjective and without definitive value. Therefore, profundity is important both for the researcher who desires to immediately engage the authentic significance of existence and for the artist who strives to articulate it through astute description.

One might, for example, consider another human being and merely acknowledge their outward appearance without ever recognizing their intrinsic existence. Similarly, we could regard someone else exclusively from our own pre-conceptual preference and prejudice. But if we encounter another human being straightforwardly from the condition of our own essential existence, we immediately discover their intrinsic identity. We find that they are not adequately represented by their appearance nor are they are we imagine or evaluate them to be. They possess a singular distinction that we recognize as unique through the perspective of our own originality of existence.

The essential uniqueness of the existence of someone else or of a phenomenon may then be carefully represented through an artistic medium of communication. Thereby, that which is portrayed is neither the physical appearance nor an emotion interpretation, but the authentic distinction.

Thus, the unique individuality of existence of someone else is poignantly experienced through direct cognition. Furthermore, this quality of recognition is the profound view of the authentic condition of another person, and unique individual is consequently very respectfully acknowledged.

13. The Essential Identity

The immediate recognition of the elemental condition of the human being, subsequently established as the perspective from which all other things are known for the intrinsic circumstances of their existence, is of primary significance. The human, elemental condition is the singularity of the individual entity and unique distinction possessed by each person. Consequently, recognized as the paramount, cognitive view-point of our constitution, through the aegis of our intrinsic identity, we are able to experience things immediately in their essential circumstances. Indeed, the authentic condition of our own existence is similarly, straightforwardly and experientially, discovered by direct engagement. Thus, we instantly realize our singular existence and confirm its significance through first-hand knowledge, and the ipseity serves us with a foundational, cognitional premise whereupon all other phenomena are similarly, elementally recognized. Thereby, from the perspective of our intrinsic existence, all things are immediately engaged in the condition of their essential significance.

The reality of the human, singular uniqueness, as the incorporeal existence of the individual, is indisputable through direct experience. Its intangible condition only becomes uncertain when we attempt to substantiate our experiential knowledge through abstract philosophy. Thereby, the intellect challenges and overwhelms the purely experiential perception, unaware that reason is a secondary faculty that operates indirectly and is only capable of surmising a situation obliquely.

A faculty cannot experience because it does not possess intrinsic identity. But physicalism pronounces that the human being is exclusively biological. As a result, identification rests solely upon idiosyncratic differences that possess no other variation one body from another. Accordingly, the individual cannot claim a particular nature but only the diversity similar to the variety of a vegetable. Or in other words, twins with identical DNA would in fact be the same person because individualism according to the materialist is confined to the body. So much for the abstract conjecture of the philosophy of nihilism, although ominously the same conviction is widely held under different names.

Only an entity is capable of direct involvement and immediate cognition. However, the faculty of reason works in isolation from experience and serves the human being by indirectly evaluating information. But the intellect is not the human identity. It functions indirectly and remotely. Therefore, definitive rationale is dependent on the reliability of the information that it manages and the quality of its performance.

The ideal kind of information, managed by the intellect with the greatest degree of certainly, is mathematical including the quantifiable assets that pertain to physically verifiable objects. Consequently, the success of reasoned assessment convinces us that tangibly founded evidence is of greater significance than experientially derived knowledge of the intrinsic condition of a phenomenon. As a result the intangible, essential existence of things is marginalized and excluded from a conventional, philosophical assessment of life because nonphysical value is non quantifiable and consequently incommensurate with this approach.

Nevertheless, through direct engagement, the human ipseity is found to exist independently of the corporeal metabolism. However, while intangible existence is empirically justified through self-recognition, nevertheless, the authenticity of physically elusive phenomena is intellectually indeterminable because the existence of intangible significances cannot be materially demonstrated. That is to say, it is beyond the capacity and function of calculation to logically assess intangible information, unless nonmaterial factors can somehow be reduced into tangibly verified calculable form. But qualities, values and intrinsic identities do not lend themselves to quantification. Thereby, intrinsic significance inevitably loses significance when numerical conversion or calibration is compulsory.

However, as we described in the previous chapter, intangible values can be physically represented through the arts, in which case they are portrayed metaphorically and figuratively. Indeed, fine art ideally reveals the intrinsic significance and distinction of a physically

131

imperceptible subject.

Nevertheless, non-physical existence remains otherwise incommensurate with the conventionally assessed, material condition. The usual manner of designation and identification is founded exclusively upon the physical appearance of phenomena.

Nonetheless, through the direct encounter of our own intrinsic distinction and a phenomenon, we exercise a different nature of cognition from that offered indirectly by the intellect. It involves immediate experience instead of the abstract and oblique evaluation of information. Consequently, it is only through direct experience that our own individual uniqueness can be definitively identified. In other words, the contention caused by the certainty of directly determined but unprovable existential knowledge rests upon the incompatibility of insight with rationale.

Undoubtedly, the further removed we are from mathematical configuration the less possible it is for the intellect to definitively evaluate information. Nevertheless, the knowledge that we seek through immediate cognition does not concern ephemeral circumstances but a greater profundity than the material semblance. That is to say, the attention of the observer remains concentrated upon the material status, but pursues the deeper significance.

Clearly, the intellect is a faculty circumscribed within a limited capability that pertains to calculation.

Consequently, exclusive reliance upon the intellect in order to ascertain the composition and structure of the entirety of existence, inevitably reduces life to the narrow extent of the physical. In other words, a worldview composed abstractly, through deduction, presents a predictably precise but sterile scenario that is thankfully, remote from reality.

The intellect functions indirectly and, consequently, it is unable to discover conditions that require the immediate, experiential cognition of the ipseity in order to be identified. Thus, it is the immediacy of the approach that is significance. Therefore, the capacity to definitively establish the nature of the existence of a phenomenon belongs exclusively to the human, essential existence and it is achieved when our authentic identity immediately engages the corporeal proportion. But the conclusions of abstract deduction and indirect evaluation in terms of immaterial value always remain uncertain through the oblique nature of their operation. Nevertheless, by direct engagement we experience the existential and qualitative significance of something, imminently.

In summary, in order to communicate something whose existence is essentially qualitative and intangible, we must use metaphorical and figurative expressions because we are describing a condition that that is indefinable in strictly physical terms. Conversely, the perceptive individual who contemplates a work of art is able to discern the significance of the content through their own inherently established experience of profundity. In other words, when a successful art piece is viewed from the perspective of the human essential ipseity, the essential significance is immediately discernible.

The use of descriptive language, as with any artistic medium, does not inevitably reveal the intrinsic content but the artist must develop the language of the particular medium and become articulate. Similarly, when something is discovered through immediate engagement, the human essence determines, through its essential condition, the authenticity of the experience. Needless to say, the perspective of the ipseity is the final arbiter of legitimacy because as the foundational significance of our existence it serves as an ultimate measure or benchmark of authenticity.

The abstractly constructed position will always pale beside knowledge achieved upon the immediate engagement of phenomena because significance rests upon the essential condition of things. Thus, we establish a familiarity with the tenor of reality by our immediate experience of the profound, and especially the direct recognition of one's own innate being. In other words we have a measure, and a contrived, abstractly fabricated interpretation of circumstances is readily evident through qualitative comparison.

Where a condition is described without the personal experience of the proponent, the account will possess little weight and seem to have a fictional ring to it. Hence, an abstract philosophical structure will be recognized as of little value compared to a position founded upon immediate experience through the aegis of the human, essential existence. The former will appear dissonant and remote from our own direct familiarity with a more profound reality.

To reiterate, the immediate engagement of a phenomenon occurs when the human essence is established as the authority of the human constitution. Thus, the human singularity of existence engages something without trying to explain or interpret it, but by contrast, experientially encounters it. We avoid interpretation, evaluation and the reliance upon pre-established intellectual or emotional conceptualization, in order that our authentic existence can confront a situation without intervention. Similarly, our emotional preferences play no part whatsoever, and the phenomenon is engaged independently of our involvement and evaluation.

Consequently, if we wish to communicate the knowledge that we have attained through immediate engagement, it helps to remain occupied in the present with the phenomenon itself, while endeavoring to articulate our experience. We thereby avoid the inevitable abstraction of considering something after the event.

Concerning the intrinsic existence of the primary color yellow, for example, we engage it immediately.

While a color exists only marginally as a physically tangible phenomenon, the essential identity is discovered experientially because it is a qualitative thing. That is, a quality cannot be fully and directly represented physically except as a distant numerical value, or perhaps hypothetically as a wavelength, which does not resemble the qualitative existence of the color at all.

Thus, the nature of the existence of the primary color yellow is described figuratively, in the same manner as any qualitative entity that is recognized only through experience, and otherwise possesses only insignificant, physical properties.

In other words, we are interested in the intrinsic identity, and we engage the color originally through the perspective of our own individual certainty of existence. Through immediacy, we recognize the qualitative significance of yellow and endeavor to communicate it. Alike to the skilled artist we require a suitable terminology in order to reveal our direct experience of something intangible, and for this purpose we now select a string of adjectives and metaphors.

Thus, we find that the identity of the archetypal color yellow of the rainbow is essentially enthusiastic but, nonetheless modest. We recognize it for this quality of existence wherever it occurs. We find it cheerful, sunny and eager, and markedly so when viewed opposite other colors.

But the depiction of the intrinsic existence of the

color yellow is only as fitting as the skill of the artist allows, yet the immediate experience of it reveals a consistency of identity that is not dependent upon how well it is communicated.

Steadily, we become aware that we are establishing a dimensional description of a color that is qualitative instead of physically founded. Instead of formulae established upon the theory of physical light within a material context, we discover the condition of the intrinsic existence, which is the profound identity.

Furthermore, our portrayal of the particular color yellow pinpoints the qualitative degree of its appearance. But if one examines two yellows such as cool lemon and warm buttercup we recognize that they share commonalities that are archetypal while they also possess individual, qualitative distinctions.

Thus, we find that yellow exists archetypally and it is recognized everywhere on the basis of the commonalities shared between all expressions of yellow. The archetypal identity of yellow is that which we recognize as common to all variations. In other words, descriptions of the essential significance of yellow fail to portray red or blue. Nevertheless, yellow of itself, possesses a unique qualitative identity and wherever it is found it will always continue to be identifiable through its condition of essential optimism and liveliness.

In order to clarify the practice whereby immediate cognition, through our human, essential singularity is able to distinguish the intrinsic identity of something, we may examine any similarly intangible phenomenon in the same manner. If, for example, we immediately engage the primary color red, again we recognize that all reds are identified as such because they are essentially composed of the same common, elemental red. That is, the elemental existence of the color is revealed through the commonalities that distinguish all reds from other colors.

Once more we discern that the archetypal red possesses an intrinsic condition, that we here describe as warmth and courage. It is not sanguine like yellow, but potent. The same myriad nuances exist that distinguish between different variations of red. Thus, warmth and courage may be subtly differentiated as intensity, or inexorable intrusion, and, as before, lightness or gravity, expansiveness and restraint, rarefaction and density, intensity and calm, describe the particular qualitative dimension that is inaccessible to a physically established depiction. However, wherever we find red we recognize the commonalities of courage and passion that identify the archetypal condition that is the essential nomen of the color.

Therefore, depending of the skill of the artist, the essential significance of a phenomenon may be portrayed. But the importance of this example is less the accuracy of the description, but most importantly, the manner whereby the intrinsic profundity of something can be individually discerned.

14. Intrinsic Significance

The actual identity of a thing is the innate distinction that specifies what it is in terms of the essential significance. Essential significance is discerned whenever our engagement of a phenomenon is immediate and original. Indeed, when we restrain thinking, presumptive understanding and partiality, inevitably our perspective alters from abstract to the straightforward view of our own existential significance. Thereby we encounter a phenomenon unequivocally without interpretive compromise.

While it remains difficult to communicate an unfamiliar condition unless someone were to possess similar experience, nevertheless, if we endeavor to experientially recognize our own singular existence, we find that the immediate cognition of everything else is predicated upon the significance of our own singularity. We silently experience our intrinsic identity and establish our own existence as a cognitive position from which to engage other phenomena.

The conventional cognitive approach does not offer definitive knowledge concerning the essential condition of things. It merely presents information about the physical appearance and substance of phenomena. Indeed, it is supposed that we might arrive closer to an identification of phenomena through analysis. However, thereby we commence a continuous reduction, revealing increasingly divided aspects each with a particular identity of its own that may even alter depending on the context in which it exists.

Consequently, if we think we can successfully identify something based upon a representational formula, in the same manner whereby any intrinsic distinction is overlooked upon a scrutiny of the separate properties, the essential significance of the whole is thereby misunderstood. Indeed, a formulation is the substitute of an actual event.

As an example, Eiweiß is the familiar German word Egg-white, which means protein. There is no doubting the biochemical complexity of protein, and therein lies the value of the term. But if we wish to describe the same substance to the unacquainted, Egg-white is a far more descriptive word, and in that sense it is more meaningful. Indeed, there are many German words in continued usage that remain richly descriptive while the English translation introduces words that are increasingly obscured by scientific formality.

We have already discussed how the qualitative dimension of existence is entirely marginalized by materialistic Western philosophy because intangible evidence is considered negligible. Indeed, the intellect cannot definitively verify the existence of incorporeal value because it is beyond its function. Therefore, the inadequacy of abstract conjecture is self-evident because of the way that the intellect and the imagination function remotely. We reason logically about a situation or a phenomenon and endeavor to envision its possible significance. But alone, through the intellect and the imagination, we can never decisively discover what the entirety of something is.

Thus, we find ourselves limited to a very narrow perspective through an approach founded exclusively upon material evidence and, consequently, we are confounded, having hindered our own cognitional progress. Through materialism we prevent ourselves from exploring the significance of our individual existence and from experientially recognizing the incorporeal distinction of our essential identity.

Nevertheless, the difference between abstract deduction and immediate cognition requires little further clarification because the distinction is represented in the language type. However, it is commonly assumed that systematic and logical reasoning offer a superior caliber of intelligence over direct experience, and it is thought that the speculative nature of abstract thinking offers the possibility of the discovery of an otherwise unexpected solution. Similarly, intellectual authority considers reliance upon empiricism to be limited because abstraction offers the advantage of theory and conjecture that may then be logically evaluated.

First of all, immediate cognition is an almost unknown approach to understanding even though it is frequently practiced unconsciously. Furthermore, abstract deduction does not offer a better understanding but merely a different methodology with alternative consequences. That is to say, immediate cognition allows the observer to recognize the profound condition of the existence of a phenomenon. In other words, what it is. But abstract rationale works remotely from the event and calculates possibilities that usually concern the purpose of things. Thereby, we typically allocate words that represent the physics of something instead of a portrait of the intrinsic nature.

Immediate experience is only significant when the human singularity of existence, that is our authentic identity, is established as the seat of the cognitive perspective. Otherwise, the engagement does not possess the weight of definitive knowledge. But, when the human essence encounters something, it meets it as it exists in and of itself which is the same state wherein we discover our own authentic identity. In other words, we cannot deduce an existential condition because it must be experienced in order to be discovered, and deduction in a calculating activity that is incongruous with immediate experience.

Similarly, existential belief is a predilection and not a cognitive practice, and consequently it does not enter the equation even though it may be apparently justified and confidently upheld. Nevertheless, it does not assist us at all in terms of definitive knowledge because it does not even have the advantage of rationalism, but must rely on revelation and conviction. Further, the object and tenets of one's belief may or may not be authentic. Indeed, there are countless denominations that contradict individual development and antagonize separate autonomy.

Immediate engagement by the respective essential significance is inherent to human intrinsic individuality, while superficiality is typical of mindlessness and indifference. Nevertheless, there are many institutions and societal norms that inhibit the awakening mind and sustain thoughtlessness. Indeed, the agencies that work against healthy individualism are not only found among the ignorant but also operate despite elite authority.

All the same, the human unique selfhood alone is able to discover, through direct experience, the existential distinction that intrinsically separates one phenomenon from every other. Consequently, the determination to advance beyond a moribund mentality of half-knowledge, and discover the profundity of things, is itself an indicator of maturation. In other words, the decision to inhibit the conventional indirect approach to understanding, engaging phenomena from the perspective of our authentic identity is indicative of awakening.

Thus, we recognize things immediately and engage them in the unaffected condition in which we find them through direct encounter. Consequently, profound directly ascertained knowledge is different from the conclusions that we establish concerning existence through our conventional faculties. Indeed, immediacy is a state of existential authenticity that is found through immediate experience and must be engaged by our essential existence in order to be known. Inevitably, from the perspective of the materialist this seems merely the subjective interpretation of an apparent condition and, consequently, it is considered indemonstrable and fictitious. The materialist would rather abstractly explain existence in terms of material phenomena because intangible information that can only be recognized through experience, cannot be logically deduced.

Therefore, the confirmation of the authenticity of a situation to the materialist is akin to the proof of an equation in the sense that the intellect works most efficiently if it can assess data in mathematical form and reduce phenomenal conditions to manageable equivalences. But the terms true and false, are not the same as real and unreal, and upon this distinction, the difference is revealed between the calculating function of the intellect and the practice of immediate experience. The intellect must strive to prove a position while immediate experience concerns the recognition of the way things actually exist. Consequently, reality cannot be demonstrated or disproved through analysis and deduction because it is the state of existential authenticity that must be experienced directly, in order to be verified.

Immediately engaged, all things are discerned by the human, essential existence as they exist elementally. In other words, superficially we are aware of the peripheral circumstances, but direct cognition reveals the entirety of phenomena. Thus, the perspective of the human, essential distinction recognizes the authentic condition of things and does not have to rely on conventional, indirect practices of interpretation.

Customarily, we endeavor to discover the nature of phenomena through the analysis and scrutiny of quantifiable properties and of their mechanical activities. But the human, essential distinction is able to ascertain what something actually is as an entity.

Otherwise stated, the physical construction and workings of a phenomenon do not reveal its intrinsic identity. They merely show how something functions. Indeed, identity is not discernible through physical operations nor discovered through an analysis of the way something works from the perspective of mechanics, chemistry or electronics, but it exists intrinsically. That is to say, the distinction of something belongs to the being and not to the doing.

Convinced of the supreme advantage of reason to establish the identity of things, we overlook the fact that the intellect, consistently, fails to do so. We imagine that we have made sense of what things are, based upon how they operate, but thereby, we find that we have philosophically interpreted the world from the perspective of function. Predictably, the results consist entirely of mechanical systems of one variety or another. Thus, we assume that whatever system drives and

145

operates an organic phenomenon is the entirety of its identity and significance. We imagine that processes, the interactions between components and the scrutiny of physical properties conclusively encompass the existential circumstances of something. But how something works is not what it is. Thus, the appearance conceals the identity of a phenomenon which exists intrinsically as the particular distinction that conveys the explication of its existence. The identity of something is what it is, not what it does or how it appears or how it functions.

A description of the identity of something must include the manner of its intrinsic existence. The physical appearance, workings and functions offer only partial representation, but fail to include characteristic expression. Nevertheless, the materialist, as we have already stated, will insist that appearance and function alone comprise the full extent of a phenomenon. But this only shows that an indirectly established, exclusively materialistic conceptualization of existence has been formulated that is at odds with directly known reality.

From the recognition of the intangible, qualitative dimension of existence through immediate experience, we further directly explore phenomena and discover that they possess an intrinsic significance that is their essential identity. It is true that material appearances primarily posses physical properties, but when we recognize propensities of behavior this belong to an otherwise elusive proportion. Namely, qualitative value and characteristic inclination are dispositions of existence which is the innate significance of phenomenal identity. That is to say, the nature of the existence of something is revealed through the manner whereby it expresses its existence.

The materialist, predictably, attributes the qualitative distinction of a phenomenon such as a color, for example, to an associative brain function and the optical quality of the eye. But the human, essential existence straightforwardly engages a phenomenon and immediately penetrates beyond the appearance to the qualitative significance. What the eye or the brain have to contribute is circumstantial, but the human essence is neither a function nor an instrument. That is to say, the phenomenal appearance anchors the attention but the human, essential existence identifies the intrinsic existence even of a color, through immediate discernment.

Consequently, attributing a numerical value to color may be convenient for practical usage but the suggestion that color is merely an electromagnetic radiation of a certain wave frequency and intensity, is typical of the inverted manner of materialistic thinking. In fact, it may be valid that electromagnetic radiation of a certain condition is colored, yet color is not found through immediate experience to resemble magnetism, radiation or waves, but it is qualitatively identified.

In the attempt to quantify color the science of

chromatics has established a way of calibration and, subsequently, presents color as if it were entirely represented through quantification. Thus, the attempted computation of something whose identity is essentially intangible, is further exacerbated when it is imagined that disconnected, consequential physical properties may be isolated and exist independently. The irony is that the abstraction and manipulation of factors that cannot exist independently of an object, involve not only something whose significance is without physical representation but also something that, in fact, does not exist separately except in the imagination. That is to say, the immediate engagement of a color does not suggest an invisible wave, a minuscule particle nor a numerical quantity or measure, but the color is found to exist as a qualitatively unique identity of a most specific singularity.

15. The Inherent Cognitive Capacity

We each possess an innate cognitive capacity that allows us to discern the nature of the intrinsic existence of phenomena. The efficacy of this ability depends upon the perspective of the individual, essential distinction that allows us ready, experiential access to the identity of things.

This is something the intellect cannot achieve because reason is a function and not an entity. As such, it works indirectly and it is only obliquely concerned respecting phenomena, endeavoring to understand them through reflection. Furthermore, reflection occurs after an event or abstractly, entertaining imaginative and hypothetical speculation.

The essential significance of the individual does not reason but remaining extant as an entity, it directly experiences phenomena. That is to say, through immediacy, the ipseity engages circumstances without preconceptual prejudice. Thus, both the cognitive perspective and the event of immediate engagement represent the critical distinction between rationale and empirical discernment. Thereby, through original observation the primary principle of the existence of something is unambiguously identified.

Discovering the elemental condition of things is significant because knowledge of intrinsic relevance provides insight into the entirety. Simply put, the human essence engages the essential meaning and discovers the intrinsic importance that is the authentic identity which precedes the physical condition. Thereby, having direct experience of the underlying circumstances the mind is able to discriminate between that which is substantive and the inessential, and therein lies cognitive liberty.

The intrinsic distinction that defines a phenomenon, is the authentic identity that determines its physical appearance. But the appearance is not the identity. The identity exists as the intangible dimension from which the appearance ensues.

If we wish to describe the intrinsic existence of a phenomenon, we find the appearance alone to be inadequate. This is because the physical condition does not reveal the intrinsic existence nor, in terms of the organism, the conceptual dimension upon which its archetypal existence is established.

For example, the conceptual dimension of an organic phenomenon resides in the commonalities that all variations possess even though individually, they appear differently. In other words, all trees are recognized as trees and an incipient biological concept is common to them all.

Similarly, while all colors are identified generally as colors, they are individually distinguished through their particular elemental distinctions. But the identity of an organism consists of the qualitative distinction of the consitution together with the application of a common archetype, and the conceptual existence of the archetype itself.

In another vein, apart from the indirectly functioning intellect it is imagined that the quality of something can be satisfactorily determined solely through the human, feeling nature. If this were the case then the qualitative dimension of existence would be evaluated according to the particular interpretation of each individual. Everyone would construe the condition of a thing differently and we would be unable to conclusively discover the inherent, qualitative distinction. Consequently, the inconsistency of interpretation through the human feeling nature cannot be relied upon to offer definitive information.

However, as we have already stated, the human being possesses as the consequence of essential individuality and our uniqueness as an entity, the capacity of direct cognition that does not concern instinctual antipathy or sentimental appeal. Objectivity of this caliber is possible because the singular nature of the essential existence of the human being does not reside within the same context as the body, nor within the physical functions. That is, the ipseity is the primary distinction of the human being, and while the body exists as the superficial appearance, the unique substantive distinction resides immanently within the same volume as the essential significance of all things.

Alternatively, the qualitative significance of a

physical phenomenon is similarly intangible, and it too occupies the same dimension as the human, essential existence. For this reason the human absolute identity is able to determine the nature of the essential identity of another phenomenon as it essentially exists. That is to say, they occupy a corresponding elementary proportion that is of greater significance than the physical because it is not only apparent but actual. Therefore, we find that the vacillating, feeling nature of the human being is not the appropriate medium through which the nuances of qualitative existence may be definitively determined, but the individual emphatic existence is.

In terms of the importance of the acknowledgement of the inherent value of something, excluding the qualitative dimension of existence from our philosophical understanding of life because the human, feeling-sentient nature inconsistently interprets it, is a poor justification for its omission. But the very existence of an exclusively physical interpretation of existence reveals an impoverished, materialistic mindset that overemphasizes the physical and marginalizes the value of the consequential.

It is extraordinary thing to grasp the repercussions of a contrived world-view that is severely weighted in favor of physicality. Thereby, we are misled into believing that the entirety of existence is composed of matter and in every sphere of experience the ramifications of materialism are found to precipitate further superficiality.

Nevertheless, it is unhelpful to replace a myopic perspective that only acknowledges the carapace of phenomena, with another belief. It would serve human development better if we each discover the substantive proportion for ourselves.

To reiterate through example, qualitative significances and the conceptual dimension of organic phenomena exist intangibly. Through immediate engagement the human, essential singularity identifies both qualitative value and conceptual relevance that is everywhere apparent in Nature.

The diversity of plant and animal life upon Earth is attributed by conventional wisdom to capricious mutation. It is imagined that diversity erupts spontaneously and that its survival suitability is randomly tried and tested by a capricious ecology. This perspective is the predicable consequence of materialistic Western philosophy because it avoids the influence of the intangible evidence that promotes speciation. That is to say, the modification of the characteristic nature of a creature initially influences the nature of form-expression.

Thus, immediate engagement reveals both the qualitative distinction of the creature itself and the biological conceptual foundation. It is found that animals possess feeling-sentience, the nature of which is also revealed in the temperamental demeanor and in a consequent physical emphasis. That is to say, the appearance follows the successive adjustments of dispositional accentuation between the creature and ecological influences. Namely, an alteration in the demeanor of the feeling-sentient nature of the creature, arises in response to change in the compound, ecological circumstances that dominate it.

Indeed, the bodily condition of the particular organism at any time is additionally an aspect of the ecological influences to which it responds. In this sense, there exists a qualitative reciprocity between form and demeanor but the demeanor of the creature also represents an aspect of the compound of influences to which the nature of an animal, its offspring and other animals adjust.

That is, ecological circumstances provoke the possibility of an adjustment in expression and consequent form gesture. Nevertheless, the consequent outward appearance is both cumulative and inheritable.

Nevertheless, we should remember that the alteration in physical appearance only concerns the extant condition. That is to say, a change in temperament will only influence a currently established constitution. The prior physical arrangement is constantly superseded by an adjusted temperamental stance or qualitative disposition reflected in the corporeal expression..

This is easy to grasp when it is recognized that even the presently established appearance still continues to be influenced through profound changes in demeanor. But the cumulation of alternative characteristic attributes establishes form definition that is subsequently adjusted through further temperamental alteration. Therefore, primordial ecology would obviously have been entirely different from recent conditions, and the original undifferentiated organic life would have been pristinely susceptible to the formative influences that promoted speciation and eventually populated every Earthly environment.

Plant life is similarly, qualitatively diverse but the ecology in the case of flora responds to direct influence because vegetation, unlike the animal kingdom, is not feeling-sentient. Nonetheless, the changes in the character of a plant are similarly cumulative. The medicinal or poisonous nature of some plants is the most obvious indication of qualitative distinction. Every herbalist, skilled chef or sommelier is well aware of the qualitative value possessed by different plants, their roots, leaves, fruits and seeds, that cannot be adequately summarized through chemical analysis.

Through materialistic bias, abstract theoretical evaluation and ignorance concerning the nature of human, essential existence, we have established a perspective towards existence that is woefully inadequate. This is redressed through the experiential recognition of the significance of human, essential ipseity and its direct, cognitive capability, whereby it is able to engage things in their elemental condition and discover the intrinsic nature of their existence.

16. The Practicable Approach

The value of the discovery of our own unique intrinsic identity is obvious from the moment that we recognize the significance of incorporeal existence. We find that the immediate cognition allows us unfettered, cognitive access to the non-material significance of things. Thus, through immediacy we engage phenomena profoundly and experience their essential, existential situation.

The less than obvious non-physical dimension of the existence of things is unapproachable through the intellect, and it must be directly experienced and discerned in order to become known. It is for this reason that the intangible significance of existence is excluded from conventional, Western philosophy or at best, mishandled and only vaguely addressed; it is feared that we may regress towards bygone superstition. But if an ideology through dogmatic narrowness impedes the means towards a better understanding of existence, and if physicalism merely reproduces the same banal explanation irrespective of a superabundance of data, it may be worth reexamining the restrictive principles that circumscribe our thinking.

The physically elusive significance and intrinsic distinction of phenomena are immediately accessible to the similarly intangible singularity of the human being. To the degree that we establish our authentic identity as our primary, cognitive perspective, we become increasingly familiar with the consequence of the non-material proportion that qualifies the appearance with meaning. Thus, we engage things directly while restraining the usual interpretative tendencies of the intellect and the feelings, and from our own incorporeal individuality, we experientially identify the inherent nature and qualitative expression.

The incorporeal dimension of existence consists of myriad qualitative distinctions of every caliber and range of emphasis. Thereby, the substantive manner through which a particular phenomenon is expressed reveals the intrinsic distinction that is the actual, descriptive identification. In other words, the most profound singularity of something is not only the material form, but the character of the expression.

The perspective of the individual ipseity offers an unusual and practical cognitional approach because the engagement is experientially immediate. Immediate cognition does not require interpretation or clarification through reason but it encounters phenomena directly and discovers the essential condition of their existence. Experiencing things as they exist intrinsically, we find that we possess a certain cognitive autonomy because we do not have to interpret or evaluate information, but we discover things as they are through first-hand engagement.

The indirect approach, through our thoughts and

feelings about something, provides only a theoretical conceptualization concerning phenomena and existence. Thus, through abstract evaluation and reflection, and preference founded upon intellectual prejudice or sentiment, we achieve ingenious explications of life when we extend our evaluation into philosophy. But immediate cognition reveals the contrived nature of our expository constructs and they are found merely to indirectly mimic reality while inflating obvious aspects at the expense of the more illusive essentials which are difficult to physically negotiate.

The intellectual interpretation of existence varies enormously depending on the disposition of the researcher and the particular perspective. The wide discrepancy in opinion is a certain indicator of the fallibility of our conventional, cognitive approach. But the view achieved through the immediate engagement of the human, essential identity, involves the direct experience of the extant condition that is more discernment of the way things actually are than merely a different perspective. Indeed, the ipseity is disinterested in theoretical constructs and conceptual models and finds the intellectual interpretation of existence to be an uncertain and circuitous approach because it does not deal with the absolutes founded upon directly experienced knowledge.

Similarly, terminology possesses associations that are misleading if the terms used have not been defined and agreed upon. They may suggest something entirely different from what was intended. Furthermore, an excess of technical language that takes a very long time to understand tends to establish an inaccessible exclusivity. Thereby, existential knowledge is assumed to be the prerogative of elite scholarship just as formerly a clerical hierarchy presumed religious entitlement.

But direct cognition is not concerned with self-importance and pomposity but involves the immediate experience of a condition wherein everything is discovered as it exists authentically. There is only one reality and, consequently, everything can be corroborated by another person who similarly experiences a phenomenon immediately from the perspective of their own incorporeal existence.

Vague and mysterious allusions are evidence of abstract constructions and emotional interpretations. Consequently, one can be certain that the condition of profundity has not been authentically experienced by the individual who portrays essential circumstances in a veiled and enigmatic manner. In fact, direct cognition requires that the intellect be restrained and emotional subjectivity be surpassed by the engagement of the human, intrinsic identity. Therefore, a superficial semblance of human singularity cannot directly encounter phenomena because it is not the authentic identity. Only an entity can experience. That is, the intellect is a function and the emotions are idiosyncratic and cannot offer decisive evidence.

If a phenomenon is directly engaged from the perspective of our incorporeal existence and discovered as it authentically exists, the experience may be difficult to articulate because intangibles, such as qualities are not easily described using physically derived terminology. The inherent and particular distinction of the color red is almost beyond description unless it is artistically portrayed, and, unfortunately, the capacity of art to articulate the intangible has become reduced through dilettantism.

But the incorporeal existence of the human being, once discovered, can experience the inherent and particular identity of for example, a color, or discover the conceptual origin of organic life and directly recognize the qualitative dimension of existence and, subsequently, strive to express the intangible. Furthermore, anyone with similar experience will recognize the legitimacy of the portrayal.

The recognition of the incorporeal existence of the human intrinsic identity is of paramount importance not only in terms of cognitive autonomy, but because we can discover how things essentially occur. We no longer have to speculate and deduce because we can confront physical appearances and discover in them a natural intrinsicality, similarly meaningful as our own unique existence.

17. Insight

Immediate engagement offers insight concerning the intrinsic significance that forms the basis of the existence of material conditions. In turn, directly ascertained knowledge of essential circumstances provides a benchmark pertaining to the nature of substantive particularity.

Consequently, when we become sensible of the intrinsic merit of things, recognizing the innate qualitative distinction and particular manner of expression through immediate engagement, knowledge of the profound extent of existence can be establish as a benchmark of authenticity. Thus, with attention consolidated in this manner, the contrived position, whether founded upon revelation, intellectual conception or as a fusion of the two, is proportionately and qualitatively compared with a definitive standard.

Substantive circumstances are discovered when the human essence immediately and impartially, directly engages something. In this sense, the human essence refers to the entity that remains when the conventional, cognitive activities are restrained and our perspective is thereby unimpeded. This is possible because the physical appearance is a secondary condition compounded by additional intangible but salient evidence that pertains to the intrinsic manner of its existence. That is to say, the essential distinction and qualitative manner of expression of a phenomenon are overlooked from a predominantly physical perspective. Nevertheless, through immediate cognition it is found that the human essence exists in the same situation and circumstances as the intangible significance of the phenomenon. Therefore, in terms of the entire identity of the object, the distinction of its existence is not found in the appearance, however finely the physical properties may be scrutinized and subsequently labelled. The intrinsic identity of a phenomenon, discerned experientially, resides in the intangible vale that qualifies the material appearance with significance.

For example, the intangible significance of a sugar-pine cone exists within the entirety of the tree manifestation and its particular, qualitative expression. Similarly, the entire existence of an exhaustive, archetypal organization is asserted by the particular tree according to a specific nature of representation. At the same time, the archetype consists of a compound of deliberate metamorphosis, reiterated locally through every detail and expression in order to establish specific functions within the entirety.

Furthermore, it is the archetypal purpose that instructs a damaged organism to repair according to the demands of an original, overall conceptualization and a more individually distinctive character. However, generally speaking, if the plant or animal is too severely compromised then the creature can no longer function as an integrated organism and must inevitably disintegrate towards unspecified biomaterial because it has become untenable as a viable entirety.

The existence of the archetypal conception of organic organization is evident to immediate cognition. Moreover, the qualitative manner of the particular representation is a further significant proportion that is similarly discovered through direct discernment.

Also, of considerable interest, is the occasion itself of firsthand engagement between the human essence and the object. That is to say, the immediate cognitive event impresses the researcher with an experience of the condition in which things exist in their multidimensional entirety. It is found that the imminently experienced state is absolutely real, while partial evidence derived merely through an examination of the physical appearance, remains only legitimate as a description of the carapace. That is, the appearance is of minor significance in terms of a comprehensive identification because of its incompleteness.

The cognitive event of immediacy is an intentional occurrence that permits direct discernment and it is further compounded in its significance because it involves the instantaneous cognition of things as they exist elementally. Additionally, the human essence engages a circumstance directly without the interference of the intellect or emotionally derived preference. Consequently, perception of this caliber involves the essential or original state of a phenomenon because such is the condition in which the entirety of something exists. Therefore, through the direct manner whereby the intrinsic human being approaches something, it discovers the primary identity.

This description does not include the familiar manner where with the intellect or the human feeling-sentient nature perceives things, nor the abstract interpretation of existence derived merely from the most readily accessible, physical evidence. Consequently, it is from the position of immediate recognition by the essential selfhood of the human being, that all obliquely derived constructions that purport to explain existence is examined and subsequently evaluated, for their authenticity.

We seldom recognize phenomena afresh and uniquely, but we bow instead to a preexisting acceptable digest. That is, we rely upon a particular, prevailing convention and accepted interpretation towards life in order to understand things. Therefore, in the case of contemporary materialism, we imagine existence to be other than it is, replacing original circumstances with a preconceived, substitute conceptualization. Consequently, we endure according to the constraints of a counterfeit philosophy.

Furthermore, if we differ at all from the accepted perspective, we do so only in terms of an alternative abstraction or prejudice. Consequently, what is often described as a unique or original position, is seldom established upon the discovery of the profound conditions of existence but commonly represents a reshuffling of the arrangement of an existing evaluation or interpretation. Therefore, the apparently original approach to something remains merely an alternative emphasis, as if a different combination of physically derived factors would elevate the significance of an exclusively materialistic approach.

Consequently, the conviction that the entirety of the existence of things consist exclusively as a physical representation, remains entrenched. For example, the proposition, maintained by modern physics, that phenomena consist of minuscule building blocks, possessed of only tacit existence, that somehow assume organization and identity through spontaneous aggregation, does not work when applied to the humanly manufactured item, yet we assume that it happens naturally.

Unfortunately, through the indirect manner in which a preconceived notion is augmented by abstract manipulation and partiality, scarcely anything is experienced in its pristine circumstances. Accordingly, the cognitional approach, wherein phenomena are engaged originally, in order to discover the elemental condition in which they exist uncorrupted by human definition and exposition, requires the abandonment of preconceptions.

However, even an alternative view is hardly

significant unless the human, incorporeal selfhood is established as the authority of our existence, and in order to achieve a unique perspective, the familiar interpretative practices must be restrained.

Unfortunately, if the straightforward approach is suggested as the means whereby we may experientially discover the intrinsic significance of things, the mainstream establishment balks. Thereupon, the suggestion is dismissed as a mere belief. Furthermore, if it is proposed that, from the perspective of the human essence, all things may be discovered in their multidimensional condition of existence, the convinced materialist scoffs and denounces the proposal as fictional. Nevertheless, while standard practices demonstrate tremendous strides in knowledge concerning the physical constituents and mechanics of phenomena, nothing but an increasingly superficial philosophy is evident in human affairs because substantive knowledge is unattainable through a scrutiny of solely material conditions.

18. The Insufficient Perspective

The consequences of a mystical approach towards the discovery of a more profound meaning to life than the material are inevitably enigmatic. In so far as cryptically ascertained information cannot be straightforwardly and empirically verified, even if we trust the sincerity of the practitioner, personally exclusive knowledge is unreliable. Indeed, irrespective of the traditional source, it is important that the objective of our research should be definitely established in order to avoid impulsive conviction.

The manner whereby a deeper perspective might be established towards existence than the corporeal, must inevitably begin with physical circumstances themselves. Thereby, the efforts of the investigator are supported by a verifiable certainty that offers a reliable point of departure. In other words, the obvious condition of things represents an undeniable circumstance that should not be relinquished but serve as a mainstay, whereupon a more insightful understanding might be developed.

The rationale of our inquiry concerns the limitations of an understanding of existence that is entirely circumscribed by material parameters and possess little significance beyond the conspicuous appearance. Materialism, as a philosophy, of itself, should not pose a challenge, but interestingly, the human being is uneasy with the menacing concept of mortality. Indeed, corporeal over-identification is at least one source of significant and justifiable insecurity.

However, either the temporal view is as well-founded as it appears, and we linger momentarily between birth and death, or mortality is real but our point of view is too narrowly confined, and consequently we fail to understand the significance of the Earthly sojourn.

Extensively, throughout this book, the emphasis has rested upon the latter proposition. Furthermore, building upon the assumption of existential ignorance because lack of profundity is commonplace, the unexceptional thesis of materialistic Western philosophy has been discovered as insufficiently justified because intangible significances are well-known but purposefully overlooked. Thus, the recognition of a sleight-of-hand makes the openminded researcher suspicious.

Consequently, the premise that suggests the possibility of greater existential significance, unperceived from a purely material way of thinking, gains increasing credence. However, the difficulty remains concerning the means of a more insightful approach that is readily accessible to straightforward inquiry.

Remaining faithful to physical coordinates, it becomes evident that everyone is already aware of physically elusive nuances that qualify material conditions with additional significance. But upon further investigation, it is found that qualitative descriptors possess even greater relevance than the physical appearance because meaningfulness is established more pertinently with the characteristic designation of something than the otherwise empty object. In this sense, it is as if the material were a shell or a husk that is only significantly inspirited according to an innate, physically elusive nature.

The qualitative significance of a phenomenon is easily ascertained. But the analogy of the sommelier helps to clarify the intended meaning. The vintner utilizes a terminology that is most explicitly suitable in order to describe a fine wine. Indeed, there are at least forty accepted terms that are used to characterize the sense experience. Yet, if the wine did not possess qualitative value, not only would the phraseology be useless, but the wine itself would exist without distinctive merit. That is to say, the wine would remain unsubstantiated and we would be unable to distinguish one thing from another.

If that were not enough, a phenomenon that is entirely without qualitative justification is also void of both significance and meaning. But quality, consequence, and relevance are all intangible characteristics that are otherwise known to exist. Consequently, materialism is dismissed as a fraudulent philosophy because it excludes the physically elusive merit of things that we experientially know to be legitimate.

Upon the incentive of this discovery, without

abandoning the material carapace for one moment, the conclusion is reached that there exists an unseen significance that pertains to material conditions. With this in mind, we explore the manner whereby the qualitative significance of something is determined. Thereby, we discover that both the sommelier and the fine artist already posses an approach whereby intangible, essential significances may be definitively discerned. The approach is immediate cognition.

19. The Human Entity

The portraitist uses the qualitative significance of a particular color in order intentionally to express a certain meaning in much the same way as the sculptor applies gesture and muscular tension in order to convey a specific demeanor. But one need not be an accomplished artist in order to practice immediate cognition, although considerable skill is required with a view to successfully representing intangible significances.

Immediate cognition is an experiential practice applicable to all material phenomena, including the human being. Thereby, one discovers, as we would anticipate, the essential consequence that underlies the conspicuous manifestation. Obviously, recognition of the essential person is of singular importance in terms of meaningful relationship as opposed to mere superficial interaction. Furthermore, through insight it is distinctly feasible to discover and distinguish between the host and the biological vehicle.

Thereby, it becomes evident that the human essence is not of the same substance as the biology, but it is subject to a different accountability and relevance that is appropriate to qualitative improvement and maturation.

Furthermore, by the same means that was applied towards the discernment of the primary human identity, insightful comprehension is applicable with respect to the universality of the human form in comparison with the very particular animal structure that corresponds with a specific nature.

For example, everything concerning the demeanor of the eagle is similarly, corporeally represented. But the disposition of the human being remains elusive and cannot be determined from the shape except in so far as an indicative potential towards a certain liberty due to undifferentiated biological structure. That is to say, the animal is bound and restricted by a specific corporeal definition that it cannot escape unless the character could change itself towards greater generality. Even so, the creature remains limited within the constraint of irreversible speciation. Conversely, the human frame remains undefined and in every respect capable of extraordinary expression.

But there is always more to discover. By way of illustration, having established the distinction between the body and the host, we can now turn our attention towards the essential selfhood in much the same way as we might examine something as equally, physically subtle as a color. Thereby, through immediate cognition, we discern the essential significance of the human quintessence and recognize, therein, the unique individual principle.

The individual quintessence, is this same principle entity that comes to the fore when we restrain conventional thinking normally expressed through

174

cerebral evaluation, associative comparison, and feeling sentience, and experientially engage circumstances directly. Furthermore, it is the quintessential significance of the human intrinsic selfhood that allows the observer to discern the qualitative expression and intrinsic distinction of all other phenomena.

The human essential singularity of existence is the authentic identity of the human being and the only distinction of the human constitution that is intransient. This is because the unique entity is not the physical appearance nor a corporeal function but the extant self. Consequently, only the human singularity of existence can immediately engage a phenomenon in terms of its essential condition. That is to say, the singular entity exists emphatically, and from that perspective alone immediate engagement is achievable.

Furthermore, when the human quintessence immediately experiences selfsame uniqueness, identification with any aspect of the human body becomes problematic because corporeality is incommensurate with the intrinsic selfhood. Thus, we find, through self-recognition, that we exist intangibly and that our individual significance remains separate from the body because it is the host and not the vehicle. That is, essential existence concerns unequivocal being and as such, it remains independent of attributes and functions because processes cannot possess an extant independence of identity of their own.

The condition of the existence of essential being is qualitatively incommensurate with anything that does not possess similarly particular distinction. Therefore, functions do not exist in the same way as entities because while they perform a task, but they are not persons. However, the intrinsic distinction of every being is discernible, and the difference between the two is thereupon clearly evident. Indeed, if we were without intransient selfhood, then every human being would share the same identity.

20. The Heart of the Soul

Attentive to the quintessential distinction, we recognize another proportion that pertains significantly to the human being. Specifically, the individual sentiment represents the qualitative timbre of the inviolate selfhood that we describe as the soul-disposition. In other words, everyone possesses a unique, intrinsic distinction that is changeless. But the human being is qualitatively amended by a particular temperamental timbre that in the animal kingdom engenders the cumulative form-expression. That is to say, the dispositional character of the soul, by analogy, is observable characteristically in Nature as an animalian expression.

The human, characteristic propensities that we establish towards circumstances, similarly represent the aggregate disposition of the soul. Thus, through the environmental ambience of the formative years, we establish propensities and temperamental inclinations that become the particular predilection that is carried forward and remains. In other words, we each approach circumstances in a particular way that is determined by predetermined inclination.

Simply put, the essential ipseity does not need correction, but the human mentality is in dire need of remediation and maturation. Indeed, the present psychology is moribund and ill-suited to a meaningful future because the soul is circumscribed by inappropriate and even regressive tendencies. Amongst the attitudes and instincts that are unsupportable in terms of human evolution, the self-first attitude is significantly dysfunctional.

The manner whereby the character of the soul is crafted is determined by the sympathies and animosities that we accommodate within the heart. Indeed, the substance of that which we cultivate and nurture influences the qualitative timbre of the soul for good or ill.

The difficulty arises when we decide that certain proclivities are no longer suitable and we wish to dispense with them. It should be straightforward and indeed it would be uncomplicated simply to abandon undesirable habits through resolution, were it not for the entrenched nature of temperament. That is to say, disposition is not superficial but woven into the fabric of the soul itself. Therefore, a particular morale is not easily dislodge because character is a factor of the expression of the human constitution.

That being the unfortunate case, it would appear that there is no remedy to the human plight and that we are each destined to live according to a particular species of predilections not dissimilar to animal instinct. But in reality, the timbre of the human soul is susceptible to amelioration, and even to the inception of a successive disposition established upon goodwill and integrity.

The manner whereby a consecutive nature may be

inaugurated within the human constitution concerns the heart of the soul.

We have already discussed the manner whereby the present moribund mentality became ingrained over time as the respective disposition, and the means of remediation is similar. That is to say, an exemplary nature must be permitted to preempt the existing inclinations through individual willingness.

Contiguously positioned to the respective heart there resides an irreproachable, dispositional archetype that represents the prospective human nature. At this point in time, the immaculate principle remains a human potential. But the successive disposition becomes realized to the degree that the individual accommodates the accomplishment of volitional regeneration through openhearted sincerity.

Furthermore, we may approach the supernal nature through openhearted sincerity in order to replenish the weary mind. Yet, the same replenishment serves also as a qualitative remediation that reorientates the human being according to a successive disposition. Indeed, if we knew this simple thing and understood what we were doing, even insurmountable circumstances would assume an alternative perspective.

TOWARDS A MEANINGFUL FUTURE
The Continuum of the Qualitative Expansion of the Soul

THE IMMANENT PRINCIPLE OF INTEGRITY AND GOODWILL
The Integration of the Principle of Virtue within the Human heart

THE EVOLUTIONARY IMPERATIVE OF OUR TIME
The Crucial Establishment of an Inspired Ethos with the Individual,
Human Heart, appropriate to a Meaningful Future

RECONCILIATION WITH HUMAN DESTINY
The Surrender of the Heart-of-the-Soul as the Expedient Approach
Towards Direct Engagement with the Immanent Exemplar of a Future,
Human Disposition

THE QUALITATIVE EVOLUTION OF THE SOUL
The Evolutionary Transformation of the Human Soul Through
Openhearted Sincerity Towards Immanent Caritas

THE SUPERNAL ETHOS
Unanimity with the Divine Nature

THE BEGINNING OF WISDOM
Knowledge through Immediate Engagement

UNDER THE AEGIS OF IMMANENT CARITAS
The Reorientation of the Human, Disparate Self-circumscribed
Mentality

THE DECEPTION OF MATERIALISTIC WESTERN PHILOSOPHY
An Exploration of the Physically Elusive Volume of Existence

THE MEANINGFUL VOLUME OF EXISTENCE
An Exploration of the Overlooked Intangible Significance of Phenomena

THE OBSOLETE SELF
Individual Uniqueness and Significance beyond Egocentrism

HUMAN SOVEREIGN AUTONOMY
The Discovery of the Human Ipseity and its Establishment as the Essential Authority of the Human Constitution

THE TRANSFORMATION OF THE SOUL
From Self-Centeredness to Sovereign Autonomy

THE IMPLICATION OF HUMAN, INCORPOREAL EXISTENCE
The Overlooked Significance of the Intangible and Qualitative Dimension of Existence

IMMEDIATE EXPERIENTIAL COGNITION
The Inherent Human Capacity of Immediate Engagement

THE HUMAN ESSENTIAL IDENTITY
Direct Experience of Intangible Significance

KNOWLEDGE THROUGH DIRECT COGNITION
The Human Conscious Individuality and Immediately Experienced Reality

184

www.ingramcontent.com/pod-product-compliance
Lightning Source LLC
Chambersburg PA
CBHW070753100426
42742CB00012B/2117